Studying Deductive Logic

Studying Deductive Logic

FRED R. BERGER

University of California, Davis

PRENTICE-HALL, INC., Englewood Cliffs, New Jersey

Library of Congress Cataloging in Publication Data

BERGER, FRED R   1937-
   Studying deductive logic.

   Bibliography: p.
   Includes index.
   1. Logic.   I. Title.
BC71.B4   162   76-23234
ISBN 0-13-858811-2

© 1977 by PRENTICE-HALL, INC.
Englewood Cliffs, New Jersey

Printed in the United States of America

10   9   8   7   6   5   4   3   2   1

PRENTICE-HALL INTERNATIONAL, INC., *London*
PRENTICE-HALL OF AUSTRALIA PTY. LIMITED, *Sydney*
PRENTICE-HALL OF CANADA, LTD., *Toronto*
PRENTICE-HALL OF INDIA PRIVATE LIMITED, *New Delhi*
PRENTICE-HALL OF JAPAN, INC., *Tokyo*
PRENTICE-HALL OF SOUTHEAST ASIA PTE. LTD., *Singapore*

To my parents, Lillian and Harold Berger, *who reared me from a state of infantile incoherence to the state I new enjoy of (partial) rationality.*

Contents

II

Alternative Approaches within Logic   *46*

III

Some Further Topics in the Philosophy of Logic   *83*

IV

The History of
the Development of Logic

A Selected Bibliography

Index

Preface

This is a book *about* logic, not a text book *in* logic. Logic texts quite properly emphasize the learning of techniques of logic. There is no substitute for actually working with logical systems and techniques. Students are interested, however, in an overview of the field; they want to know something about the nature of logic, its historical development, and the philosophical problems relating to logic. In recent years logic texts have made some effort to include more wide-ranging discussion along with the presentation of techniques. There still, however, has been no book devoted primarily to outlining these larger concerns. This book is meant to fulfill that need.

The book aims primarily to serve as a resource tool for teachers of beginning courses in modern deductive logic. It is intended to be used alongside a standard text, reading being assigned from this book as the instructor deems appropriate. In many courses time will not permit using all of this text. In a one-quarter or semester course it is probably best to use only Chapter I, parts of Chapter III, and Chapter IV. A longer course will naturally permit wider selection.

The book may also be useful in courses in the philosophy of logic, as Chapter III is a fairly comprehensive account, on an elementary level, of recent work in that field. It is also heavily annotated in order to provide guides for further reading for more advanced students.

Though intended for readers already using a standard text, some concessions have been made to those who will be reading this book alone. This is particularly the case in Chapter II, where certain techniques often covered in standard texts are outlined in this book. The reader who merely wants some acquaintance with logic would be well advised, however, to read the excellent book by Wesley Salmon, *Logic,* 2d ed., Foundations of Philosophy Series (Englewood Cliffs, N.J.: Prentice-Hall, Inc., 1973).

The bibliography has been carefully selected and annotated with beginning students in mind. There is an emphasis on books which seek to develop philosophical and historical materials. There are a great many excellent logic texts available, so the bibliography is quite limited.

It should also be pointed out that the use-mention distinction is observed by the use of single quotation marks to refer to expressions. Metalinguistic variables are also employed in a standard manner. Neither of these is explained in the text; moreover, the variables are not clearly distinguished from schematic letters (which are mere place-holders). In addition, there are some places where the single quotes and variables are used together in a way which is strictly correct only if the quotes function as devices of quasi-quotation. Though I decided these technicalities may confuse beginning students, there are introductory courses for which such refinements are in order, but the instructor will have to provide them on his or her own.

Finally, several acknowledgments of aid are in order. An earlier version of this book was prepared under a Faculty Summer Planning Award from the University of California. My assistant under that grant, Mark Boman, provided outstanding research and critical assistance for which I am extremely grateful. Dr. Edward Theil went over the earlier manuscript in great detail and his critical comments were very helpful. Professor Richard Wiebe gave me the benefit of his technical criticisms, which led to many improvements. Charles Chihara kindly spent several hours with me helping to clarify several matters. I am also grateful to Howard Pospesel and Lee Rice, who went over the penultimate draft extremely thoroughly, and made numerous suggestions and criticisms of importance. I want also to express my appreciation of the efforts of a succession of my teachers who taught me logic and also developed in me an appreciation for logic as a philosophical subject: James Willard Oliver, Morton Schagrin, Ernest Adams, Richard Cartwright, and John Corcoran. As these teachers well know, I am capable of making my own mistakes, and I claim full credit for any which remain in this text. Nancy Feiner provided speedy and accurate typing, however, which has helped reduce the number of errors, both grammatical and logical. I want lastly to acknowledge the contribution of the production team at Prentice-Hall. There are numerous ways in which production aspects of a book enhance its availability and value to students, and I especially want Norwell F. Therien, Jr. and Jamie Fuller to know that I appreciate that contribution.

FRED R. BERGER

Studying Deductive Logic

I

What Logicians Study

1. LOGIC, REASONING, AND ARGUMENTS

Students who begin a logic course normally think of logic as having a connection with reasoning or thinking. Just what that connection is, however, is not too clear. Some think of logic as the study of "how we think"; others view such a course as teaching them *how* to think, or how to think *better*. As depictions of what a *logician* studies, these conceptions are at best somewhat mistaken and at worst wholly wrong.

For example, if a student entered a course and did not already know how to think, there is no way he or she could profit from instruction. The ability to learn from instruction presupposes the ability to think. Moreover, the situations in which thinking or reasoning are involved are so diverse, and involve so many kinds of subject-matters, that the logician could hardly prescribe to students how they *ought* to think or how they could improve their thinking in *all* such situations. In addition, the techniques employed by the logician are quite abstract and somewhat complicated, so that in most reasoning situations it would be impractical to employ them.

Thus, one should not view the techniques and methods of logic as primarily designed to teach one to think better. This is not to say that one will *not* be able to employ his or her reasoning capacities better as a result of studying logic. After all, in the course of studying techniques and principles that can be applied to reasoning, one becomes aware of pitfalls and mistakes into which one can fall, and some logic courses, in fact, make explicit study of such kinds of mistakes or "fallacies"; [1] also, all logic courses give some practice in applying the principles learned to everyday sorts of examples. Reasoning better may be an important by-product of the study of logic and may be an ultimate goal that makes the study of logic useful, but it is not an essential part of the subject-matter of logic. What, then, *is* the connection between reasoning and what the logician studies?

Reasoning is an everyday occurrence. A student awakes at 9:30 A.M., remembers her logic class meets at 9:00, and realizes she will be late for class. After going out a great deal with another couple to dinners, parties, movies, and so on, at which they have always been late, a couple conclude that their friends are always late. A man comes down to breakfast, sees his wife melting butter in a frying pan, and, as she makes him eggs many mornings, concludes she is making him eggs. These are simple, relatively straightforward examples. Consider a somewhat more complicated situation. A scientist is working on a set of experiments to confirm (or disconfirm) a hypothesis in his field. He begins on a Monday morning, seeking to design the experiments in a foolproof way, so that if one set of results turns up, it will make the hypothesis almost certainly true, and if another set of results comes up, the hypothesis will almost certainly be false. He plans out the experiments on Monday morning, then goes to lunch. When he returns, he discusses his plans with colleagues, who suggest certain modifications. He returns to his office, considers what effects the changes would have, accepts some, rejects others. He begins to set up the experimental apparatus, which he does not complete until returning to work on Tuesday morning. Tuesday afternoon and Wednesday morning he spends hunting for a new house for his family. Wednesday afternoon he returns to his laboratory and discovers that no significant result is to be had from the experiments, but he cannot see why not, or how to redesign the experiments. He goes home to dinner and to bed, thinking about his scientific problem off and on. After lying awake in bed several hours, he gets a hunch that one particular feature of the design of the experiments may be the culprit, though he has no reason to think this other than a certain "feeling" about it. The next day he redesigns the experiments, sets them up, and goes home to dinner. By Friday afternoon he has significant results that confirm his hypothesis.

This example of reasoning differs from the others in (at least) the following respects: it occurred over a period of days, and it was interrupted by a succession of meals, periods of sleeping, house-searching, and so on. In their details, in fact, *each* of the examples differs from the others. Our more complicated example is more strikingly different only because it is so much more complicated. We can, however, notice the following similarities. In each case someone came to have a certain belief, and that belief resulted from other beliefs he acquired or already had. Our imagined scientist, for example, came to believe a certain scientific hypothesis to be true, because he believed that a set of scientific experiments had a particular result and not another. The late-waking student believed herself to be late for her logic class because she believed the class to have already begun, while she was still in bed.

Let us note that each of the beliefs held in our examples can be expressed in a statement: 'It is 9:30 A.M', 'I am late for my logic class', 'The experiments yield results that confirm the hypothesis'. In each case, then, we can list the statements that came to be believed and those that led to or supported the belief. In other words, in any completed reasoning process we can *abstract* from the actual process a statement that the reasoner drew as his *conclusion* and a set of statements that were the *basis* of his conclusion.

Now, suppose someone disbelieved or doubted the statement that our imagined reasoner had concluded was true, but had not gone through the reasoning process. Our reasoner might try to convince the doubter by pointing to the statements that formed the *basis* of his conclusion, hoping to get the other to believe them. In other words, he would cite these statements as *justification* for holding the conclusion. In effect, he would be giving an *argument* to show that the conclusion was true. From any completed reasoning process, then, we can abstract a set of statements that could be cited as an *argument* or basis for the conclusion. Suppose, on the other hand, we merely had a list of sentences that support a certain conclusion, whether or not they had been employed in any actual reasoning process. Those statements *could* be cited as part of an argument for the conclusion, *if* someone needed to support that conclusion. Since such sets of sentences *could* be employed as arguments, logicians simply call them arguments. It is arguments in which logicians have an interest. Let us look at some of the characteristics of arguments.

First of all, as logicians usually define them, arguments are merely lists of sentences,[2] of which one is taken as the conclusion and the others as the basis of the conclusion. The sentences involved may or may not have been a part of an actual reasoning process. Some of them may, in fact, be very unlikely to be believed by anyone. Consider the following:

> The moon is made of green cheese. If the moon is made of green cheese, the sun is a body of water. Therefore, the sun is a body of water.

From the logician's point of view this is as much an argument (and a "valid" one at that) as any that is actually employed in reasoning. The initial propositions, if true, either do or do not support the conclusion, and this is enough to make the list an "argument."

In an argument we must be able to isolate one statement that is the conclusion. Though we shall later discover exceptions, normally the others are called the *premises*. In most arguments, then, there will be some statements that are the *premises* and one that is the *conclusion*.[3] Now, as the premises are supposed to "support" the conclusion, we have a "good" argument if the premises *do* support the conclusion; otherwise, it is a poor or bad argument. Quite clearly, it is important to us to be able to distinguish good from bad arguments. As a rough characterization, which we shall qualify later, we can say that the logician's primary objective is to establish the bases on which good arguments can be distinguished from bad ones.

Suppose the logician is successful in developing criteria of good reasoning. We have already pointed out that from any example of a completed reasoning process we can abstract an argument, in the logician's sense. This will mean that if the logician is successful, we can test actual reasoning to see if the conclusion is, in fact, justified by the statements that form its basis. Thus, one connection between logic and reasoning is that logic can provide a *test* of actual reasoning. But there is more to the connection than just that. If we know what it is about arguments that makes them good ones, then we might well be able to develop techniques whereby from given statements we can deduce or infer conclusions that are supported by those statements. That is, we might be able to apply our techniques to knowledge we now have to see what further conclusions that knowledge supports. Thus, a second concern of the logician is the discovery of techniques that can be employed to *construct* good arguments—i.e., that can be used to infer, from given information, those conclusions that the information supports.

The logician's primary interests, then, are not with reasoning, but with arguments: the criteria for distinguishing good from bad arguments, and techniques for constructing good arguments. Still, there is a connection with reasoning, since, if the logician is successful, his results can be used to test actual reasoning or can be employed as an aid to actual reasoning.

Logic is an abstract discipline with important applications. This is why studying logic is much more like studying abstract algebra than it is like studying psychology. This is also part of the reason why so much of the study of logic is devoted to the learning of techniques and symbols, which, in the context of the classroom, may seem to have little practical point. It is part of the aim of this book to further the student's appreciation of the abstract, theoretical subject-matter he is learning.

2. INTUITION AND THE DEVELOPMENT OF LOGIC

Good reasoning does not await the instructions of the logician, nor does one's ability to distinguish good from bad instances. Men were doing this long before logic became a developed discipline. There are a number of reasons for this, and several philosophical theories about the nature of logic and its foundations have attempted explanations.

At the very least, it is clear that the process of acquiring a language necessarily involves grasping certain logical connections and relations among statements. One would not fully understand the meanings of 'all', 'no', and 'not' if he or she did not understand that a statement of the form 'All *A* are *B*', if true, would warrant belief in the statement 'No *A* are not *B*'. Coming to know the full meanings of the words 'all', 'no', and 'not' *involves* becoming cognizant that if all *A* are *B*, then no *A* are not *B*. Some terms of a language figure in an essential way in determining the logical relations of statements in which they occur (more on this later), and learning fully the meanings of these terms involves learning something about these logical relationships. Whatever further philosophical explanation we are to give *this* fact, there should be no initial mystery about our logical abilities as language users. We could not learn a language, or communicate with it, without at the same time learning of logical relations among statements. As will become clear in a bit, not *all* that we know about good and bad arguments is connected with the acquisition of *linguistic* competence, but it is true that a measure of logical ability is gotten in this way. This means that students who come into a logic class already are (somewhat) competent reasoners, able (to some extent) to distinguish good from bad arguments.

Of course, few people have thought explicitly about such matters; thus, most persons would be hard put to say *why* good arguments *are* good or what principles help produce good reasoning. For this reason it is common to describe the logical ability people have that is unaided by explicit instruction as an "intuitive" logical capacity, and the basis of the logical discriminations and techniques employed as "intuitions."

The fact that we all do have a logical capacity, and an intuitive ability to reason correctly, is of extreme importance to logic. Logic, as an intellectual study and discipline, develops from our intuitive logicality. By virtue of our ability to recognize obviously valid or invalid arguments we can examine examples to see what distinguishes them. Because we actually employ certain techniques in ordinary reasoning, and reject others, we can study these, seeking to make them precise, and we can discover new techniques and systematize them. To a great degree, logic consists in the attempt to make explicit what is implicit in our successful reasoning attempts—i.e., to clarify, systematize, and develop in a precise, organized way what is implicit in our intuitive logicality. The process of clarification and systematization may (and often does) result in our dropping certain of our intuitions or discovering new principles or techniques. Moreover, it may stimulate new insights or intuitions. Thus, what we come out with in the end may appear quite different from what, on an intuitive basis, we might expect, but this in no way undercuts logical intuition as a starting point.

3. DEDUCTIVE AND INDUCTIVE LOGIC

By using our logical intuition with respect to examples of arguments, we can quickly discover a very important distinction that logicians make. Consider the example of the man who comes to breakfast and sees his wife melting butter in a frying pan. His reasoning might be represented by the following argument:

> She often gives me eggs for breakfast. She has always cooked the eggs in butter in the frying pan. When she has not given me eggs, she's never used the frying pan. Therefore, she's making me eggs.

We would not hesitate to describe this as good reasoning. In fact, it is all so obvious, we might hesitate to say a husband actually *reasons* to such a conclusion in these circumstances. In any event, the initial statements provide strong support for the conclusion. Nonetheless, it is still possible for the premises to be true and the conclusion false. Suppose, for example, that the man's wife had experienced a sudden, irresistible desire for a pan-fried steak. She might, then, contrary to previous circumstances, be preparing to fry herself a steak, having already prepared oatmeal for her husband. His conclusion—that she was preparing him eggs—though supported by true statements he believed, would in fact be false. Though his reasoning was good, the conclusion was false, owing to some fact he could not know about. Though the premises of the argument provide strong ground for the conclusion, we nonetheless recognize that they do not guarantee the conclusion.

Let us consider another example—the student who awakes late for her logic class. An argument corresponding to her reasoning might go as follows:

> It is past 9:30 A.M. If it is past 9:30 A.M., then I shall be late for my logic class. Therefore, I shall be late for my logic class.

Not only can we immediately recognize this as a good argument, but we can also see that if the premises are true, the conclusion *must* be true also. We can express this a number of ways: the premises *guarantee* the conclusion; if the premises are true, then necessarily the conclusion is true; it is not possible for the premises to be true and the conclusion false.

The two examples we have considered differ in the following way. In the first example the truth of the premises makes the conclusion *probable*. That the premises are related to the conclusion in that way makes it reasonable for one to draw that conclusion, based on those premises. In the second example the truth of the premises would assure with certainty the truth of the conclusion. There is a *necessary* connection between the premises and the conclusion. In other words, the premises provide a certain basis for the conclusion. Good arguments of the first kind—in which the premises make the conclusion probable—are called inductively valid. Those in which the premises guarantee the conclusion are called deductively valid. The study of the principles and techniques by which inductively valid arguments are arrived at and assessed is known as *inductive logic*. The study of the criteria and methods of deductively valid arguments is called *deductive logic*. This book is devoted to the latter subject-matter.

One should be aware, however, that actual reasoning is not divided up neatly according to the logician's departments. Most reasoning involves appeal to *both* inductive and deductive criteria. The premises of most interesting deductively valid arguments are arrived at by inductive methods. The proper picture is that of a chain of reasoning, some parts or steps of which are justified by deductive standards. As those standards and criteria are widely different from one another, it is useful to divide up our study of logic into inductive and deductive logic.

4. VALIDITY AND LOGICAL FORM

Let us appeal once again to our intuitive ability to recognize good arguments, in order to discover something else of importance about deductive logic. Consider the following arguments: [4]

I	II
All mammals are warm-blooded.	All humans are rational.
All dogs are mammals.	All women are human.
Hence, all dogs are warm-blooded.	Hence, all women are rational.

We would all recognize these as deductively valid arguments. Brief inspection reveals something else of importance—these arguments are quite similar to one another in their structure:

All X are Y.
All W are X.
Hence, all W are Y.

If we take that structure, or form, and substitute the word 'mammals' for each occurrence of '*X*', 'warm-blooded' for '*Y*', and 'dogs' for '*W*', the result will be argument I. If, on the other hand, we make appropriate substitutions for the letters in the structure, the result will be argument II. Such a structure or form is referred to as an *argument-form*.

Let us note something else about argument-forms. Sometimes we have an argument and cannot tell for sure whether it is valid. But sometimes we *can* tell whether it is valid or not by looking at its form. Consider the following:

> Either the Pirates will win, or the Orioles will win; and the members of the winning team will get more money. If the members of the winning team get more money, the Pirates will win. Therefore, the Pirates will win.

It is not uncommon to be undecided about whether this is a valid argument. We can, however, note that it has the following form:

> (Either *P* or *Q*) and *R*.
> If *R*, then *P*.
> Therefore, *P*.

We see that the first premise asserts that *R*, while the second says that *if R, then P*. From these, we can conclude *P*. The first premise has extra information, which, in the English, may have confused us. In other words, the argument-*form* of this argument is one that obviously yields a valid argument. No matter what statements *R* and *P* (and *Q*) are, the argument that results from appropriate substitutions in the argument-form obviously will be valid. We can express this by saying that the argument-*form* is obviously valid. Recall the argument-form of our previous arguments, I and II.

> All *X* are *Y*.
> All *W* are *X*.
> Hence, all *W* are *Y*.

This, too, is an obviously valid argument-form; we can see immediately that any argument that resulted from putting appropriate terms for the letters would have to be valid. Now, this is an important discovery. We now see that we can conclude an argument is valid *because* it has an obviously valid form. Since having an obviously valid form is sufficient for it to be valid, we can conclude that it is valid by virtue of its form. Though we shall have to qualify this statement later, we can say that deductively valid arguments are valid by virtue of their form. It is, in part, for this reason that deductive logic is sometimes referred to as "formal logic."

The fact is that in our informal, everyday assessments we implicitly recognize that logical form is crucial to an argument's validity. A common way of criticizing an argument is to say, "If *that* argument were good, then so would this one be . . . ," after which a similar, obviously *in*valid argument is produced. This ploy works (when it does) because we recognize arguments to have similar forms, which are obviously valid, or invalid, as the case may be.

Of course, this way of working is tricky business, because any argument can have *several* forms. Argument I, above, was said to have the form:

> All *X* are *Y*.
> All *W* are *X*.
> Hence, all *W* are *Y*.

But, it also has the form:

> *P*
> *Q*
> Hence, *R*

This latter form is obviously invalid, and this fact presents us with a puzzling situation. An argument can have a form that is obviously valid, and another form that is obviously *in*valid. Let us add quickly, however, that this does *not* mean the argument is both valid and invalid. We noted that having an obviously valid form is *sufficient* for the argument to be valid. Now, if an argument *is* valid, then the premises guarantee the conclusion; and, if that is the case, the argument is *not* invalid. So, if it *also* has an obviously invalid form, this fact shows nothing at all about the validity of the argument. The upshot is that having a valid form is conclusive of the validity of an argument, while having an invalid form is not conclusive of the invalidity of an argument.

5. VALIDITY, TRUTH, AND SOUNDNESS

Consider the argument-form:

> All *X* are *Y*.
> All *W* are *X*.
> Therefore, all *W* are *Y*.

We recognize intuitively that any argument resulting from substitutions in this form is valid. This will mean that the following is a "valid" argument:

III

All men are women.
All children are men.
Therefore, all children are women.

Recall, we said that in a deductively valid argument the truth of the premises guarantees the truth of the conclusion. By this we meant that *if* the premises are true, then the conclusion *must* be true. Argument III is valid in this sense, for, *if* those premises *were* true, the conclusion would be true. Of course, the premises are not true and could not be true. For this reason we would probably hesitate to say that this is a perfectly good argument. We know that all the statements comprising it are false; and we know that we are *not* justified in accepting the conclusion based on those premises, since we recognize them to be false.

Let us take up another "argument":

IV

All carnivores eat meat.
Some carnivores eat dogs.
Therefore, some dogs eat meat.

Argument IV consists of true statements. Nonetheless, we would not accept this as a perfectly good argument, since the premises do not guarantee the conclusion. We can very well imagine circumstances in which the premises were true but the conclusion false—e.g., if all dogs became vegetarians. Since we can imagine such circumstances, it is possible for the premises to be true and the conclusion false. One would not be justified in accepting the conclusion based on those premises.

Normally, we engage in reasoning in order to arrive at, or settle upon, beliefs—i.e., in order to gain what we take to be knowledge. A piece of reasoning will be regarded as good if, on the basis of what is known, one is justified in accepting the conclusion.[5] Now, the examples we have considered show us that at least two aspects of the reasoning process are necessary for justified beliefs. The first example shows that the statements employed as the basis of the reasoning must be true; the second shows that the premises employed must, indeed, support the conclusion. The justifiedness of belief in the conclusion will be a function of the truth of the premises *and* the relation between the premises and the conclusion.

The first example demonstrates something else of great importance.

We were able to conclude of argument III that it is deductively valid, even though we know the premises are not all true. Our ground for being unwilling to accept the argument's conclusion is that we know it, and the premises, to be false. This means that the quality of the reasoning, and thus its validity, is *independent* of the truth of the premises. To see this even more clearly, consider that we could easily come up with an argument that has premises and conclusion from a subject-matter we know nothing about and still be able to recognize valid arguments involving that subject-matter. You should have little trouble recognizing the following as valid, even though you may not know whether the statements in it are true or false:

V

All well-formed formulas in Hilbert's first-order logic system are finite in length.

All sentences of standard sentential logic are well-formed formulas in Hilbert's first-order logic system.

Therefore, all sentences of standard sentential logic are finite in length.

We can express this fact about validity in another way. We have repeatedly said that a valid argument is one in which the premises guarantee the truth of the conclusion. We also have said that this means that *if* the premises are true, then so is the conclusion. Thus, in a valid argument, there is a certain *relation* or connection between the premises and conclusion: if the premises have a certain property (being all true), then the conclusion has a certain property (being true also). This relation is a conditional relation—*if* something were true of the premises, *then* something would be true of the conclusion. A bit of reflection should assure you that a conditional relation of this type can obtain irrespective of whether the condition is in fact met. 'If I flip the switch, the light will go on' can be true whether or not I have actually flipped the switch. 'If I shall marry Jane, she will be my wife' can be determined to be true, without knowing whether I shall marry Jane. Logicians have a special name for this relationship. It is called the *implication* or *entailment* relation. A statement, or set of statements, *implies* a statement if, and only if, it is not possible for the first statement, or set of statements, to be true while the last statement is false. *A* implies *B*, if and only if it is not possible for *A* to be true while *B* is false. A statement implied by others is said to be a *logical consequence* of the others. If *A* implies *B*, then *B* is a logical consequence of *A*. The relation of implication is the most important subject of logic.[6]

Deductive logic is concerned with the criteria and techniques of valid argumentation. Thus, it is concerned with a certain relation that can obtain among statements, *irrespective of the actual truth or falsity of those statements.* The logician, then, is not concerned with whether or not the statements he deals with are true or false, nor need he be concerned with the concept of truth itself. Two important qualifications, however, must be made to this statement.

Given the way in which we have characterized a deductively valid argument, if it is possible for the premises of an argument to be all true, while the conclusion is false, the argument is *not* deductively valid. This means that we can show an argument is *not* valid by citing circumstances, imagined or actual, such that the premises are all true and the conclusion is false. Thus, if we know that the premises of an argument are all true, and that the conclusion is false, we can conclude the argument is not deductively valid. Similarly, if we can imagine circumstances in which the premises are all true and the conclusion is false, we can conclude the argument is not deductively valid. Consider our previous argument IV. We knew the premises and conclusion were, in fact, true. We then imagined that all dogs became vegetarians. This is highly unlikely, but certainly imaginable, and therefore possible.[7] In that case the premises of the argument would be true while the conclusion was false. It is possible, then, for the premises to be true while the conclusion is false, so the argument is not deductively valid. This is, indeed, a common way of showing that an argument is not valid: we provide a *counterexample* to the claim that the argument is valid in which we show it is possible that the premises are true and the conclusion false. In this way the logician can have *some* interest in the truth or falsity of the statements he deals with.

The second qualification to the earlier statement about the logician's concern with truth and falsity has to do with a certain class of true and false statements. Consider the statement: Either the book is on the floor, or the book is not on the floor. A quick look tells one that this statement *must* be true (unless there is some equivocation in meaning). We can determine this is a true statement merely by inspecting its structure or form:

Either *P* or not *P*.

When this is the case, we say the statement is *logically* true. Contrast this example with another: The book is on the floor and the book is not on the floor. Here, we can determine merely from the form of the statement that it *cannot* be true (supposing there to be no ambiguity in the meanings of the terms). Statements of this kind are said to be *logically false* or *contradictory*. Both kinds appear trivial, of course, since there are almost no contexts in ordinary reasoning in which they usefully occur.[8]

They are, however, of very great importance to logicians; thus, to the extent that logicians are interested in logical truth and falsity, they have an interest in truth and falsity.

Our central point in this section has been that the validity of an argument consists in a relation between the premises and the conclusion that is not totally dependent on the actual truth or falsity of the sentences in the argument. If an argument *is* valid, *and* its premises *are* true, of course, then the conclusion is true also; and, if we know these facts, we are justified in accepting the conclusion. An argument that is valid and does have true premises is called _sound_. Obviously, every sound argument is valid; but not every valid argument is sound (consider our example III). For the most part, then, the deductive logician is concerned with the criteria of validity and is not concerned with the soundness of arguments.

There is a point of some importance that we have ignored thus far, and which most logic texts do not fully clarify.[9] We have spoken as if an instance of reasoning from premises to conclusion were always perfectly in order so long as the argument involved was valid and had true premises. In one respect this is correct. If we know that our argument is valid and has true premises, then we know the conclusion must be true. But *some* arguments involve our *deducing* the conclusion from the premises. This kind of argument—sometimes called a *proof, demonstration,* or *derivation*—shows us *that* the argument is valid. Let us consider an example. The following is a valid argument:

(1) I shall visit my parents if, and only if, my car is working all right.
(2) Either the mechanic fixed the car or my car is *not* working all right.
(3) The mechanic fixed my car if, and only if, he got my note.
(4) I shall visit my parents.
Therefore, (5) The mechanic got my note.

Now, if (1)–(4) are all true, the argument is valid and sound. But someone might well doubt that the premises guarantee the conclusion. In other words, he or she may need to be shown *that* the argument is valid. One way to do this would be to deduce the conclusion in a series of steps from the premises. With respect to the above argument we might proceed as follows:

Premise (1) implies that:

(a) If I visit my parents, then my car is working all right.

Since (4) says I shall visit my parents; that, together with (a), implies:

(b) My car is working all right.

(2) says that *either* my car is *not* working all right *or* the mechanic fixed it. Since the car *is* working, he must have fixed it. So:

(c) The mechanic fixed the car.

(3) implies that if the mechanic fixed the car, then he got my note. Well, since he fixed it, he must have gotten my note. Thus:

(d) (5) is true.

This sort of process is perfectly familiar in ordinary reasoning and is more like what we call "reasoning" than the mere presentation of premises and a conclusion. Sometimes, of course, to justify a conclusion to someone it is sufficient simply to show that certain premises are true. Often, however, we need to be shown also *that* the premises imply the conclusion, and we usually do this by deriving the conclusion from the premises.

The principles that govern deduction are thus an important subject for the logician. We shall discuss this when we take up "Logical Systems and Techniques" in section 7 of this chapter. Systems of deduction are of interest not only because they provide tests in logic; they are also important to the extent that they mirror actual reasoning processes.

6. THE AREAS OF LOGIC

Logic as customarily taught and studied has a number of distinguishable departments and areas. It is quite common for logic texts to have chapter headings reading: *Sentence Logic, Quantificational Logic, Predicate Logic, Syllogistic Logic.* It is useful to the student to know something about the ways in which logic can be divided up and thus about the range of kinds of topics with which logicians are concerned. It will also help sharpen the student's understanding of the nature of logical relationships.

We have already considered examples of valid arguments that illustrate different branches of logic. Recall the argument:

> It is past 9:30 A.M. If it is past 9:30 A.M., then I shall be late for my logic class. Therefore, I shall be late for my logic class.

We can exhibit the important logical aspects of this argument in the following argument-form:

1

A
If A, then B.
Therefore, B.

Clearly any argument that has this form will be valid. If we restrict our attention to argument-forms, we can note that each of the following is obviously valid.

<table>
<tr><td>2</td><td>3</td></tr>
</table>

2	3
Either A or B.	All X are Y.
It is not the case that A.	All W are X.
Therefore, B.	Therefore, all W are Y.

Earlier, we said that deductively valid arguments are valid by virtue of their form. Any argument that results from replacing the letters in these three argument-forms will be valid. There is, however, something misleading about this. Suppose that in argument-form 3 the word 'all' had the meaning of the word 'some'. Arguments that had that form would not be valid. In other words, we have supposed that recognizable expressions in English have their ordinary meanings in English. If they did not, the argument-forms we otherwise take to be obviously valid might be rejected. This shows, at the very least, that the occurrences of the English expressions in the displayed argument-forms play an essential role in determining their validity.[10] These expressions in our argument-forms may be regarded as *logical constants;* they are crucial to the determination of the validity of the argument-forms in which they occur, and they are assumed to have a given, determinate meaning, unlike the other symbols in the argument-form: the 'A's, 'B's, 'X's, and 'Y's. It happens that various branches of logic can be distinguished by the kinds of logical constants that enter into argument-forms. Let us consider the three argument-forms displayed above.

a. Propositional Logic

If we attend to our sample argument-forms, we come to notice some striking similarities between 1 and 2, and differences between 1 and 2 considered together, as contrasted with 3. In 1 and 2 we can obtain fullfledged arguments by replacing the capital letters which stand alone with sentences. For example, if we replace each 'A' in argument-form 1 with the sentence 'the light is on' and each 'B' with the sentence 'the switch has been flipped', the result will be a valid argument. Similarly, with respect argument-form 2, if we replace each occurrence of 'A' with 'the man brought books' and each occurrence of 'B' with 'the man brought candy', the result is a valid argument. This is *not* a feature of argument-form 3. If we replace the symbols 'X', 'W', and 'Y' with sentences, the result is nonsense—merely a series of English words that do not make sentences. On the other hand, we *can* replace these letters with terms, rather than sentences, and get meaningful arguments. That is, we can replace the letters with words that refer to kinds of things or characteristics and properties of things, and the result will be an argument. Replacements could be such expressions as 'boy', 'red-headed', 'unmarried males', 'recipients of honors', 'whales', 'members of the Olympic club', 'owners of Jaguar cars', and so on. We cannot, of course, use these replacements in argument-forms 1 and 2.

This sort of difference forms part of the basis for distinguishing two major branches of contemporary deductive logic. The first two of our sample argument-forms involve logical relations based on connections between sentences or propositions. It turns out that a number of expressions, such as 'if ___, then ___', and 'either ___ or ___', are parts of valid argument-forms requiring sentences as replacements. Others are: 'It is not the case that ___', '___ and ___', '___ if, and only if, ___'. This means that a large number of arguments that are valid are so by virtue of logical constants that connect, or are attached to, sentences. The study of the logic of this class of arguments is referred to as *propositional logic* or *sentential logic.*

Propositional logic, for a number of reasons, is often the first branch of logic studied. It is relatively natural and easy to learn, and the presentation of a logical system for sentences or propositions makes a good introduction to the study of more complicated branches. There is a further advantage to beginning one's study with the logic of propositions: many ordinary arguments are propositional in nature; thus, with the learning of a set of simple logical techniques, the student is quickly able to deal with a large body of arguments.

Let us notice some further features of propositional logic. We have pointed out that the logical constants occurring in such arguments connect, or are attached to, full sentences. This means that they enable us to compound new statements from old ones. The connective 'and', for example, can be written between two sentences, and the result is itself a sentence. (Of course, we may have to make alterations in punctuation or case.) Similarly, if the blanks in the expression 'If ___, then ___' are filled in with sentences, the result is a new sentence. Consider the following sentence-form:

Either *A* or *B,* but not both.

This has the feature just noted—if we replace the letter symbols with sentences, the result is a new sentence. Let '*A*' be replaced with the sentence 'I shall go to South America this summer' and let '*B*' be replaced with 'I shall go to Europe this summer'. The result is clearly a new sentence:

> Either I shall go to South America this summer, or I shall go to Europe this summer, but not both.

Suppose it is true that I shall go to South America in the summer, but not to Europe. Well, clearly, the compound sentence we constructed will be true. Likewise, if I shall go to Europe, but not to South America, the new, compound sentence will be true. But if I shall go to South America *and* I shall go to Europe, the new sentence will be false. Thus, the truth or falsity of the sentence-parts of our new sentence determines the truth or falsity of the whole. We can tell whether the compound sentence is true or false simply by knowing whether the parts are true or false. The truth or falsity of the compound sentence is a function of the truth or falsity of its constituent sentences. Logical constants that are used to make compound sentences, the truth and falsity of which is a function of the parts, are called *truth-functional* connectives. Propositional logic deals with truth-functional logical connectives. Thus, propositional logic is truth-functional.

It is important to be aware that not all sentences that have others as parts are truth-functional. Each of the following is a sentence that has another as a part:

> I believe the earth is round.
> Jones knows that Smith is the milkman.
> Smith said that the earth is round.

In each case, merely knowing that the embedded sentence is true or false would not necessarily be enough for us to know whether the whole sentence is true or false. Whether someone believes something, knows something, or said something is not completely determined by the truth or falsity of the statement said to be believed, known, or said. I can *believe* the earth is round whether or not the earth is round. I can *say* that the earth is round whether or not the earth is round. Smith may be the milkman without my knowing it. Of course, it may be that if Smith is *not* the milkman, then it cannot be true that Jones knows that Smith is the milkman. The second sentence displayed above can then be said to have a *truth-functional aspect*, since, if the embedded sentence is false, so is the entire sentence. But if the embedded sentence is true, the larger sentence may still be false, so the truth-value of the part does not completely determine the truth-value of the whole. These sorts of sentences are therefore said *not* to be truth-functional. We shall discuss the treatment of such sentences in Chapter III, section 4.

b. Quantificational Logic

Let us look again at argument-form 3. We noted that the letter symbols in it must be replaced with terms—nouns, noun-phrases, adjectives, and so on—rather than sentences in order to obtain arguments. The logic of arguments, the validity of which turns on having an argument-form of this kind, is sometimes called *term* logic. Other features of this argument-form are worth noting, however. If we concentrate on the logical constants that occur in it, we discover that each involves a reference to quantities of things—*all* of a certain kind of thing are said to have a certain characteristic, or to be a certain kind. Alternatively, we could say that *some* or *none* of a certain kind possess that property. Clearly, many valid arguments contain such logical constants. In addition to argument-form 3, consider the following:

4	5
All X are Y.	No X is Y.
Some W are X.	Some W are X.
Therefore, some W are Y.	Therefore, some W are not Y.

These are obviously valid argument-forms, in which the logical constants that play an essential role in determining their validity are such terms as 'all', 'some', 'no'—i.e., expressions that relate to amounts. For this reason this branch of logic is often referred to as *quantificational* logic.

So far, we have not examined in detail the sorts of terms that can be used to replace the letter symbols in these quantificational argument-forms. Nor have we said very much about the nature of the sentences that result from replacements in these argument-forms. Attention to these matters brings out some noteworthy features of quantificational logic.

First of all, we can note that all of the statements involve characterizing things of certain kinds as possessing or lacking some property or other. 'Some boys are not red-headed' characterizes some boys as not having red hair. Expressions that refer to properties are called *predicate terms* or simply *predicates*. In each of these sample sentences two expressions are used to characterize things. This is brought out more clearly if we paraphrase these sentences as follows:

Anything that is a boy is red-headed.

and

At least one thing is a boy and is red-headed.

Quantificational logic, then, involves predicates in an essential way. In place of the 'X's, 'Y's, and so on in the argument-forms go predicates such as 'boys' and 'red-headed'. For this reason quantificational logic is as often referred to as *predicate logic*.[11]

It is helpful to look further at the kinds of predicates that occur in sentences. The simplest case is that in which an individual object is said to have a given property—e.g., 'John Smith has red hair'. Or, as we have seen, a class of things can be said to be characterized in a certain way: 'All bachelors are unmarried'. In addition, a statement can assert of things that they are characterized by standing in a certain relation. Consider the following examples: 'John is taller than Mary', 'Smith hit Jones', 'John stood between Smith and Jones'. The predicates in these sentences are known as *relational* predicates.

We can capture the notion of a relational predicate in a visual way. Consider first the predicate 'has red hair'. We can construct a sentence-form for it in the following way: '___ has red hair'. In saying this is a sentence-form, we mean that if we put an appropriate word or phrase in the blank space, the result is a sentence. If we treat 'is taller than' as a predicate, then a corresponding sentence-form would be '___ is taller than ___'; i.e., we would have to put in *two* blanks that must be filled in. A relational predicate, then, is one, a corresponding sentence-form of which has two or more blanks. (Notice that 'stood between' requires three blanks.)

In the paragraph above, I was careful to write *a* corresponding sentence-form for a predicate, because it is clear that in a given sentence we could regard the predicate in several ways. For example, we *could* say that in 'John is taller than Mary', the sentence predicates the being taller than Mary of John. As unnatural as that may sound, it is somewhat more natural than saying that it predicates the taller-than relation of John and Mary, considered in that order. In other words, we could say that the appropriate sentence-form for the statement is: '___ is taller than Mary'. Since there is only one blank, the predicate is nonrelational. If we think of sentence-forms as bringing out the logical structure of a sentence, then the latter form may be thought of as bringing out less detailed structure, as it does not indicate visually that there is more than one reference to an object.

Now, there are in fact some valid arguments the validity of which turns on the more detailed relations. That is, we cannot show these arguments are valid unless we analyze the predicates involved as relational. It thus happens that quantificational logic or predicate logic can be further divided according to whether it deals with arguments in which the predicates are all treated as simple, or one-placed predicates, or whether the detailed structure of relational predicates is brought out. In the first case we have *simple quantificational logic* or *monadic predicate logic;*

in the latter case we have *general quantificational* or *polyadic predicate logic*. The development of polyadic predicate logic is very important, since a great many simple, obviously valid arguments cannot be demonstrated as such by means of the techniques appropriate to either propositional or monadic predicate logic. To cite one such example: All husbands are men. Therefore, all wives of husbands are wives of men.

Most courses in modern symbolic logic study propositional and predicate logic, and the student can rightly regard these as the basic areas or branches of logic. In this book, propositional and predicate logic will be called *basic logic*.[12] Other divisions are, in fact, additions to, variations of, or alternative ways of presenting basic logic. Let us consider a few examples to see how this is done and to get a picture of the range of branches logic has.

c. Identity

In our discussion of predicate logic we pointed out that the statements dealt with ascribe a property (perhaps very complex) to some thing or class of things. When developing symbols for use in a logical system for predicate logic, it will be useful to have symbols for particular things and for properties or characteristics.[13] It will be necessary also to have symbols for the logical constants—'all', 'some', 'if __, then __', 'either __ or __', and so on. A typical set of symbols would use lower-case letters— '*a*', '*b*', '*c*', . . .—to represent particular objects, and capital letters— '*P*', '*Q*', '*R*', . . .—for properties. Thus, we might symbolize the sentence 'John has red hair' by '*Pa*', understanding '*a*' to refer to John and '*P*' to represent 'has red hair'. A relational predicate usually is simply symbolized by attaching two or more lower-case letters to it. To symbolize the statement 'John is taller than Mary' we might write '*Tjm*'. '*T*' stands for 'is taller than', and '*j*' refers to John, '*m*' to Mary. Now consider the following argument:

VI

Mark Twain wrote *Huck Finn*.
Mark Twain is Samuel Clemens.
Samuel Clemens wrote *Huck Finn*.

No one who thought about it would have trouble seeing this is a valid argument. But we cannot show this in the typical predicate logic. Given the symbolic devices indicated, we can represent the first sentence with no difficulty; it could be '*Wmh*', letting '*W*' stand for the relation of being the writer of a certain book. But what are we to do with the second statement? Normally, 'is __' is a predicate-form. By putting a characterizing term or phrase in the blank, we get a predicate, either monadic or polyadic—e.g., 'is red-haired', 'is the father of Mary', 'is between John and Mary'. If we do this with the second proposition of argument VI, the predicate is 'is Samuel Clemens'. Suppose we construct a symbolic argument-form along these lines. We shall let '*W*' represent being the writer of and '*S*' represent being Samuel Clemens; '*m*' will refer to Mark Twain, '*s*' to Samuel Clemens, and '*h*' to the book *Huck Finn*. We get:

$$
\begin{aligned}
&Wmh \\
&Sm \\
&Wsh
\end{aligned}
$$

Nothing about this form shows the validity of the argument; in fact, the techniques of predicate logic would not show it to be valid. Let us consider a more promising approach. Suppose we regarded the second proposition as asserting a *relation* obtains between Mark Twain and Samuel Clemens: the relation of being identical.[14] This may sound very odd, but it is promising because there are two naming expressions in the sentence, each of which refers to an object. If we use a relational predicate, we can, symbolically, bring out this feature of the structure of the sentence. If we let '*I*' be the identity relation, we get:

$$
\begin{aligned}
&Wmh \\
&Ims \\
&Wsh
\end{aligned}
$$

Once again, however, nothing about the *form* displayed reveals the validity of our original argument. The reason is simple. The validity of the argument in fact depends on the special features of the relation of identity and the meaning of '*I*'. Given our understanding of what it means to say of x and y that they are identical, we understand that if x wrote a certain book, then, necessarily y wrote that book; or if x is red-haired, then y is red-haired, and so on. Now, we saw a parallel situation when we introduced the notion of a logical constant. We saw that the validity of arguments in propositional logic turned on the meaning of such expressions as 'if ___, then ___', 'either ___ or ___', and so forth. And, in predicate logic, we saw that the use of the expressions 'all' and 'some' is crucial in determining arguments in which they occur as valid. The argument-forms we determined as valid contained these terms, which were understood to have determinate meanings. By analogy, then, we can conclude that identity, or the word 'is', when it functions to indicate an identity, functions like a logical constant. It is in virtue of the identity of Mark Twain and Samuel Clemens that we can conclude that Samuel Clemens wrote *Huck Finn*, if we know that Mark Twain wrote *Huck Finn*. If, then, we add the 'is' of identity, or some symbolic equivalent, to our set of logical constants, we can then devise a logical system that can demonstrate the validity of argument VI. If we use '=' to mean "is identical with" or "is the same as," this argument can be symbolized in more perspicuous form:

$$Wmh$$
$$m = s$$
$$Wsh$$

Something like this is normally done in predicate logic. The system has a new logical constant added to it, which warrants arguments of the sort we have considered. The expanded system is then called *quantificational logic with identity*, or *predicate logic with identity*.

d. Modal, Epistemic, Deontic, Tense Logic

Most of the further branches of logic are additions to basic logic in much the way illustrated. They involve introducing new logical symbols to the system for basic logic, which warrant a new range of arguments. As logic widens in this way, a great many more kinds of arguments can be dealt with by the logician. Such further developments include *modal* logic, *epistemic* logic, *deontic* logic, and *tense* logic. A brief characterization helps to show the kinds of arguments dealt with.

Modal logic involves the concepts of possibility and necessity, introduced as asserted of statements, i.e., a new logical constant is introduced which means "It is possible that," and which is written before sentences. Usually ' $\Diamond$ ' is the sign for this new constant; thus, if 'P' is a sentence, 'it is possible that P' would be symbolized: $\Diamond P$. If we allow '$-$' to mean "it is not the case that," we can represent 'it is necessary that P' by '$-\Diamond -P$'. Modal logic can then be employed to deal with arguments, the validity of which involves these notions. There are, however, severe problems with this branch of logic, as there is great disagreement about the nature of the concepts of necessity and possibility, and there is a great disagreement about what arguments involving these notions ought to be taken as valid.

Epistemic logic and *deontic* logic raise disagreements quite like those involved in modal logic. Epistemic logic is the logic of such terms as 'knows that' and 'believes that'. Deontic logic involves such constants as 'it is permissible that' and 'it is obligatory that'. Though these three fields are highly controversial, they can be quite fruitful philosophical tools. For, by developing logical systems based on various interpretations of the basic terms, we learn better the consequences of the philosophical positions associated with these interpretations, and we are in a better position to assess them. Moreover, we can sharpen and clarify those philosophical positions through the attempt to devise a logical system that accords with their philosophical insights.

We should add that epistemic and modal logic are sometimes said to be kinds of *intensional* logics. We shall discuss what this means in Chapter III.

Finally, we can mention logical studies and systems that deal with arguments containing references to time, as in such statements as 'Philosophers sometimes confuse their readers', 'It rained in Chicago yesterday', and 'Jim and Deidre were married on June 18, 1960'. Some philosophers hold that these studies are relevant to various problems in philosophy and science. Moreover, there is a connection with modal logic. One way of interpreting a statement of the form '*A* is possible' is that it asserts '*A* is true at some time or other', while '*A* is necessary' asserts '*A* is true always'. (Such interpretations were advanced by a group of ancient logicians known as Megarians.) Systems of logic that incorporate temporal reference are known as *tense* or *chronological* logics.[15]

e. Higher-Order Logic

One further extension of basic logic should be mentioned here because of its great significance, although it is very difficult to explain the nature of its innovations on basic logic without going into technical detail. This further extension of basic logic is called *second-order logic*. Basic predicate logic is thus referred to as *first-order predicate logic*. (And there are orders beyond second-order.) Very roughly, the central addition second-order logic introduces amounts to the following. In first-order predicate logic we normally talk of *objects* and their properties and relations. The symbolic equivalents of 'all' and 'some' in such a system are said to *range over* things—all things of a certain kind are said to possess a property, or some things are said to be of a given kind. In higher-order logic the symbolic equivalents of 'all' and 'some' are permitted to range over properties. We can then talk about properties and the properties of properties. This is sometimes done even in ordinary discourse. Each of the following statements can be taken to ascribe a property to a property, or to state a relation between properties:

> Loyalty is an admirable quality.
> Cleanliness is next to Godliness.
> Avarice is loathsome.
> Being honest is better than being clever.

Now this may seem like a small addition to first-order logic, but it is important for two reasons. First, if we make this addition to first-order logic, we can define the identity relation. Basically, such a definition says that:

> Any objects *x* and *y* are identical if, and only if, any property that *x* has, *y* has also, and vice versa.

The second advantage is that we can define certain properties that have the properties of the natural numbers (0, 1, 2, . . .). Thus, in a sense, we can *define* the natural numbers. With certain further additions we can derive almost all of elementary arithmetic! [16] Because of this possibility, some logicians and philosophers claim that arithmetic can be "reduced to" logic or can be treated as a branch of logic.

Higher-order logic is somewhat controversial, however, primarily on two grounds. First, the proper interpretation of the additional symbolism it introduces is somewhat unclear—the same symbols seem to have two different functions. The second objection is that higher-order logic assumes the existence of special mathematical entities—sets; thus, the name 'higher-order logic' is a misnomer, since this theory smuggles in not-purely-logical notions. Philosophers who raise this sort of objection thus claim that the "reduction" to logic is illusory; higher-order logic is *not* logic.[17] Whatever one's attitude about the "logical" status of higher-order logic, however, the results achieved with it at least show a close affinity of logic and mathematics; with the addition of certain concepts to basic logic, large portions of mathematics can be formulated.

f. Class Logic, Aristotelian (Syllogistic) Logic, Set Theory

Beyond what I have called "basic logic" (i.e., propositional logic and first-order predicate logic), the other branches of logic we have considered have all resulted from additions to basic logic. Sometimes one sees references to other branches of logic that are *not* to be construed in this way, but rather as alternative ways of presenting portions of basic logic. Two such branches of logic are commonly referred to in the literature—*class logic* and *syllogistic* or *Aristotelian logic*.

The expression "class logic" most often refers to a portion of the modern theory of sets. The basic concepts of this class logic (it is often taught *as* set theory in "new math" courses) can be defined in monadic predicate logic, and all its results derived within this branch of logic. Class logic is thus an alternate way of presenting a portion of basic logic. Though, historically, class logic did not develop *as* an alternative to monadic predicate logic, it *is* an alternative to a portion of basic logic in the sense that all its results can be derived within basic logic.

A similar relationship is true of syllogistic logic and monadic predicate logic. All results obtainable through the techniques of syllogistic logic are, in fact, obtainable through the techniques of monadic predicate logic; thus, syllogistic logic can be regarded as an alternate way of presenting a portion of monadic predicate logic. This is a somewhat startling fact, since syllogistic logic had its beginnings in ancient times with the work of Aristotle,[18] received its ultimate refinements in the late nineteenth century, and, with the exception of the medieval period, was *the* method of presenting logic until well into the twentieth century. We shall trace its development, and that of modern symbolic logic, in a later chapter. Here, we shall briefly indicate what syllogistic logic is, along with its limitations.

Basically, syllogistic logic deals with arguments, the constituent sentences of which are called *categorical*. There are four kinds of categorical statements, often referred to as **A, E, I,** and **O:**

A: All *A* are *B*.
E: No *A* are *B*.
I: Some *A* are *B*.
O: Some *A* are not *B*.

A *syllogism* is an argument composed of three categorical statements, two of which are the premises, the last of which is the conclusion. The development of syllogistic logic has consisted in large part in developing rules by which to determine when a syllogism is a valid argument. In a categorical sentence the expressions that replace '*A*' and '*B*' in the **A, E, I, O** forms are called *terms*. The traditional rules for the syllogism were limited to arguments in which no more than three terms occur. The following is an example, with the terms underlined:

All men are mortal.
Some Americans are men.
Therefore, some Americans are mortal.

The three terms involved are: men, mortal, Americans. Later developments of syllogistic logic involved a technique of diagrams—overlapping circles—which can be used to test the validity of arguments composed of categorical propositions. Such diagram methods, however, are extremely cumbersome when more than three terms are involved. This is not a difficulty in modern predicate logic. Moreover, any argument that is testable in the traditional logic can be tested in predicate logic, though the reverse is not true. Thus, traditional logic must be regarded as a *portion* only of contemporary monadic predicate logic.[19] We shall discuss the differences further in our chapter on the history of logic.

Finally, we should mention something called *set theory* or the *logic of sets*. Though the elementary part of set theory can be treated as an alternative presentation of monadic predicate logic, its most powerful parts require the introduction of a new constant or symbol, used in asserting that an object is a member of a set. In the logic of sets we do not say that John Smith has the property of being red-headed; we say he is a member of the set of red-headed objects or persons. A set is just any group or class or aggregate of things. But a *set* of things need not be an actually collected group; it can be objects *thought of* or mentioned as a group. Thus, *any* objects may be brought together as a set. For example, there is the set of the following objects: Erica Jong, my copy of Quine's book *Methods of Logic,* the Empire State Building, the number 7. These are diverse "objects" brought together arbitrarily, not as possessing a given characteristic. For this, and other reasons,[20] being a member of a set is not the same thing as having a given property. Thus, the introduction of sets, and the membership relation, involves a *new* concept, not merely an alternative to a portion of basic logic. The new concepts are not regarded as being a part of logic by some logicians.[21] Set theory, in their view, is more properly thought of as a branch of mathematics than a branch of logic. On the other hand, its development has gone hand-in-hand with the development of recent symbolic logic. For this reason, aspects of this development will be discussed in the chapter on the history of logic. Moreover, many logicians *do* regard set theory as a branch of logic.

Set theory has great importance, since most of mathematics can be formulated and derived within it, and the logic of sets is presupposed in most presentations of the various theories within mathematics. Advanced set theory can also be used to accomplish the uses of higher-order logic. Set theory, of the type needed to express number theory, includes not only sets of individual things, but also sets of sets—i.e., sets the members of which are sets. It is (at least) in this respect that it goes beyond what is taught students in high school as set theory. Numbers can then be "defined" as sets of sets that obey the laws of number theory. As this is, *in effect,* what is done in most higher-order logics (since properties are interpreted as sets), some logicians prefer to dispense entirely with higher-order logic and straightforwardly adopt a fully articulated set theory. It must not be thought, however, that set theory is without its disagreements. There are a number of different set theories with different advantages and disadvantages.

7. LOGICAL SYSTEMS AND TECHNIQUES

Earlier we said that to a great extent, the development of logic consists in the attempt to clarify our basic logical intuitions, to systematize them, and to extend their application. Now, this is a vague characterization of part of the business of logic. We can clarify these functions by saying a bit more about how a *system* of logic might arise and what functions it performs. Our discussion, however, will describe only one *kind* of logical system (known as "natural deduction"); in the next chapter we shall discuss another kind.

We have seen that the material with which logic deals is arguments, and that arguments are composed of sentences or statements. We have also seen that the *forms* of those arguments and sentences are crucial in the determination of valid arguments *as* valid. Thus, one important systematizing function of logic is to clarify the *kinds* of sentence-forms that are important in valid arguments. This is furthered by developing systems of logic dealing with the various kinds of logical concepts. Thus, we have systems of *sentential logic, monadic predicate logic,* and so on. At the outset of its development such a system will pick out the basic logical constants that make up that branch of logic.

The second basic step in developing a logical system is to indicate the basic rules of inference to be employed within the system. The idea of a *rule of inference* is simple enough. Earlier, we were willing to say of a given argument that it is valid because it has an obviously valid form —i.e., because *any* argument of that form has premises that guarantee the truth of the conclusion, if they are true. In other words, a reasoner would not be making a mistake in reasoning from those premises to that conclusion. Now, the drawing of a conclusion from given premises is called an *inference* of that conclusion from those premises. In effect, we have said that an inference is justified only if the premises and conclusion involved constitute a valid argument. (Of course, validity may not be enough if a *demonstration* is needed.) We have also said that the validity of an argument turns on its form. This means that accepting an inference as deductively justified involves accepting a certain *pattern* of argument as valid. We can express this as follows: accepting an inference as deductively justified involves accepting a rule that from premises of a given form, one can infer a conclusion of a given form.

Suppose, upon examining a piece of reasoning, we conclude its corresponding argument has the following form:

If *A,* then *B.*
A.
Therefore, *B.*

By accepting the inference of the conclusion from those premises, we have accepted a rule that from premises of that form, a conclusion of that (displayed) form may be inferred. Obviously, any time we accept as valid a given argument-form, we can describe a rule that sanctions inferences from premises of that form to conclusions of that form. Thus, we can regard every valid argument-form as having an associated *rule of inference* that sanctions reasoning from premises of a given form to conclusions of a given form. Now, suppose we could do a study of valid argument-forms in order to list in a rule book the rules of inference we can associate with them. Such a rule book might be useful in the following ways. First, if we had a piece of completed reasoning, we could test its acceptability by seeing if its constituent argument or arguments would be sanctioned by the rules. Second, if we had reached a point in reasoning where we were not sure what conclusions to draw, we could refer to the rule book to see what inferences would be justified from premises of the kind at hand.

A system of logic is meant to do just this sort of thing. It systematizes logical knowledge by bringing together in an explicit fashion rules of inference associated with a given branch of logic. Such a system relies for its development on our logical intuitions concerning the validity of arguments; its ultimate utility consists in the fact that by having such a system to be applied according to explicit rules, we are enabled to test and draw inferences in cases where we might otherwise have been unsure. By making the rules of inference explicit and bringing them together in a list of rules, we make it possible to take an argument and, with no further reference to intuition, determine the argument as valid (or not) by checking each part against the rules. Such a procedure is quite analogous to doing arithmetic by reference to the tables and rules of addition, multiplication, and so on. A logical system, when sufficiently developed, makes it possible to *calculate,* much in the way we calculate in arithmetic, whether arguments are valid. Such a system—for this reason and others— is often referred to as a *calculus.* A typical logic text will thus title its section on sentential logic as "The Sentential (or Propositional) Calculus" and its section on predicate logic as "The Predicate Calculus."

We should note a further point about rules of inference and systems of logic. In deductive logic we concentrate on arguments in which there is a necessary connection between the premises and the conclusion—if all the premises are true, then, necessarily, so is the conclusion. Any rule of inference that is acceptable in deductive logic, then, must be what is called *truth-preserving.* This means, simply, that from true premises it permits us to infer only true conclusions. It should never be possible to use the rule properly and to infer from true premises a conclusion that is false. Now, there are in fact infinitely many possible rules that are truth-preserving and that could, therefore, be adopted in a system of deductive logic. Normally, we develop a system by choosing rules of inference that are naturally employed in everyday reasoning, which are sufficiently numerous to make the application of the system easy, but not too numerous to make it difficult to keep track of. Systems developed in this way are sometimes referred to as *natural deduction* systems.

The idea of *calculating* in order to determine the validity of arguments is not, however, restricted to the development of a logical system replete with rules of inference. In fact, other devices and techniques have been developed to deal with arguments and their validity. To see what they are like, let us consider one. Suppose an argument has the following form:

> Either *A* or *B*, but not both.
> Not *A*.
> Therefore, *B*.

The treatment of this argument clearly falls within sentential or propositional logic. The first premise is what we have called *truth-functional*. The truth or falsity of the compound proposition is completely determined by the truth or falsity of the parts. The sentence is true if *A* is true, or if *B* is true; it is false if both are true and if both are false. We can display these facts in a table:

	A	*B*	Either *A* or *B*, but not both
(1)	True	True	False
(2)	True	False	True
(3)	False	True	True
(4)	False	False	False

The first horizontal row of the table tells us that if *A* is true and *B* is true, then the compound sentence is false. The second row tells us that if *A* is true, and *B* is false, then the compound statement is true. We can construct a similar table for the second premise. It would appear as follows:

	A	Not *A*
(1)	True	False
(2)	False	True

This table tells us that if *A* is true, the compound is false, and if *A* is false, the compound is true. Now, let us return to the argument. It is valid if it is not possible for both premises to be true while the conclusion is false. Our tables display for us the conditions under which these statements are true or false. There are two such conditions for the first premise to be true, displayed in horizontal rows 2 and 3. The second premise is true, however, only when *A* is false. Thus, the only possible way *both* premises can be true is under the conditions displayed in row 3 of the first table. But the table shows us that in that case, statement *B* is true. Of course, B is the conclusion of the argument. We can see this more clearly by combining the tables:

A	B	Either A or B, but not both	Not A	B	
(1) True	True	False	False	True	
(2) True	False	True	False	False	
(3) False	True	True	True	True	
(4) False	False	False	True	False	

Only in row 3 are both premises true, and the conclusion is true. Thus, by referring to these tables (known as *truth-tables*), we can show that it is not possible for an argument having this form to have true premises and a false conclusion.

Still further techniques for testing validity are available in propositional logic, and even different methods have been developed within predicate logic. As we shall see, these techniques (and others) are available also for answering a wider range of questions than merely whether an argument is valid or not (e.g., the truth-table technique can be adapted to determining whether or not a proposition is a *logical truth*).

The various techniques within logic are sometimes classified according to whether they involve such concepts as truth and falsity, or whether they refer solely to the symbols and their interrelationships. Truth-tables, for example, quite obviously depend on the notions of truth and falsity. Such tests involve depicting circumstances that would make compound statements true or false. Such circumstances may be thought of as "models" of the possible truth-conditions, and tests that involve such considerations are therefore called *model-theoretic*. Tests that involve only manipulation of the symbols are most clearly exemplified in systems of deductive proof and are therefore called *proof-theoretic*. The deductive systems described in Chapter II are proof-theoretic techniques. (Model-theoretic techniques are sometimes called *semantical*, while proof-theoretic techniques are described as *syntactical*. This terminology is explained in Chapter II.)

8. METALOGIC

One does not often run across the expression 'metalogic' in textbooks, though it is a part of logic that is of great interest to logicians; moreover, most texts, even the most elementary, contain some metalogic and have problems or exercises calling on students to demonstrate important truths in metalogic. As we shall see, it is almost unavoidable that this should be the case.

When we began discussing the nature of deductive logic, we talked somewhat about the kind of relation that must obtain between premises and conclusion for an argument to be deductively valid. In so doing, we were seeking to clarify a basic concept to be used in discussing arguments. We also found it useful to distinguish an argument's *validity* from its *soundness*. This was another basic concept to be employed in talking about arguments. At another stage of our discussion we found it useful to pick out those compound statements that are *truth-functional*. Here, we defined an expression that applies to a property of propositions. In effect, we began to clarify and define more precisely a set of concepts or terms to be utilized in talking about arguments and their constituent propositions.

Once we have a set of logical concepts, we can discern relations among them. For example, it is obvious that every sound argument is valid; on the other hand, an argument can be valid but not sound. Suppose we define *a denial of a statement* as follows: a statement *A* is *a denial of a statement B* if, and only if, it is necessarily the case that *A* and *B* are opposite in truth-value—i.e., it is necessary that if *A* is true, *B* is false, and if *A* is false, *B* is true. Suppose we consider the class of statements that are logical truths and those that are logical falsehoods. We can easily show that every logical falsehood is a denial of every logical truth. Such an argument might go as follows: A logically true statement is one that *must* be true, since 'logically true' is defined as meaning "necessarily true." Thus, it is true that if we select any logically true statement and any logically false statement, it is necessarily the case that the logically true statement is true and the logically false statement is false. From this it follows that it is necessarily the case that those statements are opposite one another in truth-value. To say this is to say that the logically false statement is a denial of the logically true statement. Thus, we have an important metalogical truth: every logically false statement is a denial of every logical truth.[22]

The activities we have just described and illustrated are examples of what we are calling "metalogic." Two of the most important tasks of logic are (1) developing and clarifying the basic concepts to be employed in dealing with arguments and statements, and (2) discovering important relationships among them. To a great extent the logician is as interested in developing *these* aspects of logic as he is in developing a logical system itself or in applying his techniques to arguments. By developing these aspects of logic, the logician can work out a *theory* of logic, in which the important properties of arguments and statements can be discussed and through which they can be better understood.

Moreover, the metalogical results that can be proved often turn out to have great significance for the development and application of the techniques and systems in which the logician has an interest. Let us work out one example that shows this clearly.

To begin with, we must define several terms. A *conjunction* of sentences is a sentence that is the result of writing 'and' between sentences (and making appropriate adjustments in punctuation and capitalization). So, if *A* and *B* are sentences, we get a conjunction of them by writing '*A* and *B*'. A *conditional* sentence is a sentence that results from writing 'If ___, then ___', where the blanks are filled in with the original sentences. If *A* is a sentence, and *B* is a sentence, a conditional can be formed by writing: 'If *A*, then *B*'. Now, for any argument, we can construct what is called *a corresponding conditional*. This is done as follows.

Suppose our argument has three premises, *P*, *Q*, and *R*, and the conclusion is *S*. It would look like this:

> *P*
>
> *Q*
>
> *R*
>
> Therefore, *S*.

We can construct a conjunction of the premises as follows:

> (*P* and *Q*) and *R*.

Using that conjunction, we can then construct a corresponding conditional of the argument as follows:

> If (*P* and *Q*) and *R*, then *S*.

We can explicitly define the notion as follows: a statement is *a corresponding conditional* of an argument if, and only if: (a) the statement is of the form 'If *A*, then *B*', and (b) *A* is the premise or a conjunction of the premises of the argument, and (c) *B* is the conclusion of the argument.

Now, using a metalogical argument, it can be proved that an argument is valid if, and only if, a corresponding conditional is logically true. This is a very significant result, because it means that if we can develop a technique by which we can test to see whether a statement is logically true or not, then we can also use that *same* technique to test arguments for validity. All we have to do is to construct a corresponding conditional of the argument and test *it* to see if it is a logical truth. If the conditional is logically true, then the argument is valid; otherwise, the argument is not valid.

We must discuss a further kind of study that is part of metalogic. In fact, logicians more often think of this further set of concerns as metalogic than the topics we have already picked out. This is the study of the properties of, and relations among, the logical techniques and systems themselves. Some examples of work of this kind within metalogic will show the kinds of matters this area of logic deals with, and its significance.

We earlier introduced the notion of a *truth-table* for a statement, and we actually employed truth-tables to show that a certain argument-form is valid, and, hence, that any argument having that form is valid. In so doing we began, in a rudimentary way, to develop a technique for testing arguments for validity. We could easily fill out the procedure in greater detail and describe it sufficiently so that it could be readily applied to a wide range of arguments. Such a procedure can help us decide whether an argument is valid; thus, it is called a *decision-procedure*. We have a full decision-procedure for the validity of arguments if we can determine for any argument whether or not it is valid by applying that procedure in a mechanical, step-by-step way, and if that procedure always will provide an answer in a finite number of steps. Obviously, if we could develop such procedures, they would have great importance, since we could theoretically dispense with intuition and insight in testing arguments and apply our procedures in a mechanical way; indeed, we should be able to program a machine to do this work for us.

Now, validity is a property of arguments. It is not the only property or relation for which we desire tests. As we have indicated, the truth-table technique can be adapted to test whether sentences are logical truths. We can define the notion of a decision-procedure in a general way:

> A decision-procedure for a property ϕ is a procedure that yields a "yes" or "no" answer to the question of whether something has ϕ, which procedure is mechanical and necessarily yields an answer in a finite number of steps.

In saying the procedure is mechanical, we mean it has rules that tell us at every step what to do for the next step. One of the most important concerns of logic is that of finding decision-procedures for the various important logical properties of statements and arguments. Given that importance, a bit more should be said about decision-procedures.

Obviously, decision-procedures for validity are of first concern to the logician. We earlier spoke of the truth-table technique as a decision-procedure. Actually, this is somewhat misleading, since it suggests that we can take any argument and test it for validity using truth-tables. This is not the case. Arguments that require the symbolic devices of quantificational logic to bring out their logical features cannot be shown valid by means of truth-tables. For example, the obviously valid argument below cannot be shown such using truth-tables:

All whales are mammals.
Some vertebrates are whales.
Therefore, some vertebrates are mammals.

Since this is the case, it is wrong to describe the truth-table technique as a decision-procedure for validity, since there are some arguments about which it does *not* yield an answer concerning their validity. Still, truth-tables *can* be employed as a decision-procedure for validity *within propositional logic.* If we think of the symbolic devices of propositional logic as a kind of shorthand language, then any argument can be symbolized in the language of propositional logic. An argument, then, is *valid in propositional logic* if, and only if, it can be shown valid when symbolized in the language of propositional logic.

Now, truth-tables *do* provide a decision-procedure for *validity in propositional logic.* Given any argument at all (supposing there to be no ambiguity in meaning, and so on), we can determine in a mechanical way whether or not it is valid in propositional logic. Of course, as we have seen, we cannot conclude that an argument is not valid if we show it is not valid in propositional logic. It *may* be valid in some other area of logic; i.e., it may be possible to show it is valid using the devices of a further branch of logic. Also, it should be obvious that if an argument is valid in propositional logic, then it is valid. To say an argument is valid in propositional logic means that it *is* valid *and* that this can be shown through the techniques of propositional logic.

Is there a general decision-procedure for validity—one that applies to basic logic generally? The answer is that there are several decision-procedures for propositional logic, and for monadic predicate logic, and for certain kinds of arguments in polyadic predicate logic, but there is no decision-procedure for all of predicate logic. Indeed, there is a crucial proof available (given by Alonzo Church) that there *cannot* be a decision-procedure for all of predicate logic! Obviously, such results in metalogic are of tremendous theoretical importance.

We should note also, however, that though we may lack a full de-cision-procedure (in the sense defined), it may be possible to develop useful, partial tests for validity (and other properties). For example, we described earlier how a system of logical deduction can be developed with the use of rules of inference. Such systems can be constructed for predicate logic in general. If each rule is, in fact, truth-preserving, then such a system can be used as a test of validity in the following way. If we have an argument and are able to construct a deduction of the conclusion from the premises according to the rules of the system, then we can conclude the argument is valid. This should be obvious. If the rules are truth-preserving and each inference in our deduction is justified by one of those rules, we have, in effect, shown that if the premises are true, then so is the conclusion.

Such an inference system cannot be employed as a decision-procedure, however, for these reasons: (a) there is no mechanical way of coming up with a deduction for valid arguments—doing so is a function of our luck and ingenuity; (b) if we do not come up with a deduction of the conclusion from the premises, this may mean only that we have not tried hard or long enough; thus, failure does not warrant the conclusion that the argument is *in*valid. Such a system of inference for predicate logic can be used as a test of validity, since any argument that meets the test is valid, but it cannot be used in a decision-procedure, since no set of rules governing its use is either mechanical or effective; i.e., we do not get a definite "yes" or "no" answer for every argument in predicate logic— only in special cases can we say definitely of an argument that it is not valid using that method alone.[23]

Of course, if we reflect on our conception of a deductively valid argument, a test for showing invalidity may occur to us. A valid argument is one in which it is not possible for the premises to be true and the conclusion false. Thus, if we can show of an argument that it *is* possible for the premises to be all true and the conclusion false, then we can conclude the argument is *in*valid. Let us consider an example, one that exemplifies a common mistake in reasoning. Suppose we have the following argument:

> If I pass logic, then my father will give me a new car.
> I shall not pass logic.
> Therefore, my father will not give me a new car.

We can easily construct a story that includes circumstances making the premises true and the conclusion false. Suppose my father promises to give me a new car if I pass any one of the courses I am taking, one of which is logic. Then it will be true that if I pass logic, my father will give me a new car. Suppose that I shall fail logic but pass the history course I am taking. Then, the second premise of the argument will be true as well as the first, but the conclusion will be false. The scenario is possible; thus, the argument is not valid; it is possible for the premises to be true and the conclusion false.

Now, this sort of procedure illustrates a mode of argument very common in metalogic—the method of proving a statement false by giving a *counterexample*. In the above, we showed that the statement that our sample argument is valid is false by giving an example of circumstances in which the premises are true and the conclusion false. More commonly, counterexamples are given to statements of the form 'All *A* are *B*' or 'If something is an *A*, then it is a *B*'. We can give a counterexample by citing something that is an *A* but not a *B*. Similarly, we can disprove a proposition of the form 'No *A* are *B*' by citing something that is an *A* and also a *B*.

We can discover quite a few facts and falsehoods in metalogic by consideration of counterexamples. As an illustration, consider this statement: If an argument is valid, then it has true premises and a true conclusion. We can show this statement is false by giving an example of an argument that is valid but does not have true premises and conclusion. We earlier showed, using truth-tables, that any argument having the following form is valid:

> Either *A* or *B*, but not both.
> Not *A*.
> Therefore, *B*.

The following argument has that form and is thus valid:

> Either men are horses, or men are dogs, but not both.
> It is not the case that men are horses.
> Therefore, men are dogs.

Though valid, the argument has a false premise; thus, it is a counterexample to the statement that if an argument is valid, then it has true premises and a true conclusion.

We must bring out more explicitly one final kind of concern that falls within metalogic. The logical systems that we construct can themselves have important properties in which logicians have an interest. We have already mentioned one such: whether or not the system can be used in a decision-procedure for validity. Another is *completeness*. One sort of completeness obtains when the system is such that, given any argument that is valid within that area of logic, there is a way, using the system, of showing it is valid. We should note that a system might be complete without there being a decision-procedure for validity using that system. In that case we would know that, given any argument valid in that system, it can be shown such in the system, but there would be no *mechanical* way of coming up with the proof. Another property of a logical system that is highly desirable is that it be *sound*. This means that it not permit one to infer a conclusion from given premises that is not a logical consequence of those premises; i.e., it not certify as valid arguments that are not valid. (The student should note the difference between a sound *argument* and a sound *system*.)

The study of logical systems and their properties is a very important part of metalogic, and the systematizing function of logic is very much furthered by such a study. Some of the most important aspects of this study are best pursued, however, by the construction and study of logical systems quite different from the *natural deduction* type logical systems we have so far described. These other kinds of systems, called *axiomatic logical systems*, are characterized by starting with certain sentences (called *axioms*), which are taken as the starting points for deduction, and with a very sparse set of inference rules, which are utilized in deducing from the original set of axioms further sentences (known as *theorems*). The student is probably familiar with axiom systems through his study of high school geometry. In a later chapter we shall discuss in greater detail both natural-deduction and axiomatic logical systems.

9. PHILOSOPHICAL THEORIES ABOUT THE NATURE AND BASIS OF LOGIC

Throughout this discussion the reader may have felt a certain uneasiness about the whole enterprise that has been described. Since the entire structure of logic is built upon our logical intuitions, the student may well wonder how we get these, what justification they have, and on what grounds we are justified in accepting a logical system developed in this way. After all, is it not possible for logical intuitions to differ? Might not the intuitions of persons in other cultures differ from those of Westerners? These legitimate questions call for a discussion of the role of intuition in logic and the foundation or rationale of logic as we understand it. Needless to say, these issues have taxed some of the greatest of minds, and we cannot hope to provide the student with definitive answers. Some discussion of positions taken by philosophers, however, will help us understand the role of intuition in logic. Let us consider our logical intuitions.

Since logical intuitions can differ, it may well seem that they provide a shaky basis for establishing a logical system. Perhaps some kind of *logical relativism* is true; i.e., logical systems can be justified only relative to the intuitions of the persons who employ them. If people disagree intuitively, it may appear that there can be no basis for judging between them.

Now, the fact is that proceeding on the basis of what, intuitively, seems a truth or principle of logic has consequences that we can trace out. If, upon utilizing such a principle, we "run into trouble"—e.g., deduce contradictory statements—then we have a ground for rejecting that intuition. An example of this took place in the development of set theory. Intuitively, it had seemed obvious that for any specifiable property, there is a set of things that have that property. This proposition, known as the *principle* or *axiom of abstraction,* was shown by Bertrand Russell to lead to a contradiction. This can be shown in elementary fashion. Consider a property that some sets have—the property of being a member of themselves. The set of all sets that have more than one member has more than one member, and so it is a member of itself. Now, some sets have the property of *not* being a member of themselves. The set of ball-point pens is not itself a ball-point pen and so is not a member of itself. Now, consider the set of all sets that are *not* members of themselves. If it *is* a member of itself, then it is *not* a member of itself. If it is *not* a member of itself, then (given the way it is defined) it *is* a member of itself.

Such a result has led to rejection or modification of the principle of abstraction. An intuitively self-evident statement that was used as a basis for set theory came to be rejected because its consequences were shown to be disastrous. Thus, there *can* be some basis for accepting or rejecting those propositions or principles that intuition suggests.

Still, this will not satisfy a skeptic, or a proponent of logical relativism, for what the example shows is that disputes over logical intuitions can be adjudicated only if there is agreement *somewhere*—i.e., on further intuitions or principles of logic. In deducing our contradiction, we employed principles of inference that had to be agreed to, and we had to accept that no principle that leads to a contradiction is an acceptable principle.

As a practical matter, such an objection from the logical relativist must be frivolous in the extreme. For one thing, we can be assured there *is* such agreement at various points; if there were not, communication among persons would not be possible. A prerequisite for communication is that the truth-conditions of assertions be relatively stable. But this prerequisite would be defeated if whenever someone asserted a sentence of the form 'It is the case that *P*', he might also be willing to assert 'It is *not* the case that *P*'. We could never be sure what he was saying about the world.

The thesis of logical relativism is also unpalatable from a practical point of view, since all developed fields of knowledge presuppose the principles of logic. Thus, rejecting the soundness of standard systems of logic on the basis of logical relativism would be a hard pill to swallow, since the doubts it would cast would infect every science we know.[24]

Nonetheless, from a philosophical point of view, some further account is needed that could explain *how* we have come to such extensive agreement in our intuitions, and with what *justification* we may rely on them. We shall turn, then, to some prominent philosophical answers to these questions.

At least four theories attempt to answer one or both of the questions we have raised. It is best, however, to rephrase these questions before explaining the theories. A convenient way of expressing our questions is as follows: (a) how do we arrive at, or come to know the laws of logic? [25] and (b) what is the basis of the laws of logic; i.e., what is it that makes them true and in what way are they true?

The first theory we shall refer to as the *empiricist* view. This kind (1) of theory holds that the laws of logic are generalizations based on our experience: from the particular experiences we have we infer a general principle about all experience. Such a generalization is thus called an "inductive" generalization. The English philosopher John Stuart Mill is usually associated with this theory, as he held that the truths of logic and mathematics are inductive generalizations. A similar view was maintained by the American pragmatist philosopher John Dewey. Dewey held that in the process of acquiring beliefs—a process Dewey termed "inquiry"— men come to employ certain principles that control the inquiry. These principles (not always *consciously* applied) tend to fix habits of conducting inquiry. As the purpose of inquiry is to arrive at stable beliefs, principles of inquiry will be rejected to the extent they fail to do so—e.g., if they lead us to a belief that is upset by subsequent experience. Logic, then, consists (in part) in the study of those principles of inquiry that have held up through experience.[26]

According to empiricist positions, the "laws of logic" are derived from experience and owe their truth to their comportment with experience—i.e., are true by virtue of their according with experience. Such theories have seemed objectionable to some philosophers, since, on this view, there is nothing *necessary* about the laws of logic; it seems possible on such a view, for example, that some proposition should be both true and not true, or that it could be true that if A, then B, and that A, but that it might still turn out that not B. We seem to know *independently* of any further experience that these are not possible.

The second theory to be mentioned we will call *realism*. Realism (2) holds that the laws of logic are necessary truths about the nature of reality. Thus, one version of the law of non-contradiction—nothing is both A and not A (in the same respect)—is a necessarily true statement about the general features of the world. It asserts a general feature of all objects whatever. Gottlob Frege, a German who was one of the most important figures in the history of logic, was an adherent of the realist position as was the earlier German philosopher-logician, Gottfried Leibniz. Leibniz held that the laws of logic are true of any possible world and, thus, are necessarily true of reality.

Characteristically, realists explain our coming to know the laws of logic as accomplished through the exercise of reason. We do not generalize from experience; we "see" by reason that these laws *must* be true. Because such a theory of rational insight—the capacity of the mind to recognize logical truths as necessary merely by reflection on them—has affinities to the theory of knowledge of Plato, realism is sometimes referred to as "Platonism" in logic.[27]

A third set of theories can be termed *psychologism*. Such theories hold that the laws of logic are the "Laws of Thought." A mathematician generally identified with this approach was the Englishman for whom Boolean algebra was named, George Boole. One of Boole's most famous works was *An Investigation of the Laws of Thought*. In it he maintained that logic is a science of the mind, the ultimate goal of which is to illuminate the "nature and constitution of the mind" by discovering the laws that govern the mind's "operations."

Now, this suggests that logic is a *descriptive* science, concerned with how the mind works. The further suggestion is that, as a science of the mind, logic might proceed by generalizing from extensive study of the way in which the mind works. Such a view would, indeed, be a form of psychologism, and many who write of psychologism in logic mean a theory such as this. It faces the obvious objection that, as *descriptive* statements about how people think, the laws of logic are clearly false, since people make far too many mistakes in reasoning for these "laws" to be even approximately true. This was *not*, however, Boole's theory. Logic, according to Boole, is not a science of inductive generalizations from study of more and more instances. The laws of logic are recognized as true and as *certainly* true when presented to the mind. A single instance can be sufficient for the mind to recognize them as necessarily true. They are not empirical generalizations requiring further confirmation in experience.

Now, it is not entirely clear in what sense the laws of logic are laws of the nature and operations of the mind in Boole's theory. The laws of logic *are* obtained by "observing" the operations of the mind, but they are recognized as true immediately upon observation. The laws arrived at are *standards* for the operations of reasoning, recognized as such by the mind reflecting on itself. Boole's theory is thus a *form* of psychologism, since it regards logic as a study of the operations of the mind that formulates laws for the operations of the mind. On the other hand, the theory also contains elements of realism, as the laws of logic are recognized as true by rational insight.[28]

Immanuel Kant, the great German philosopher, also held that the laws of logic are "laws of thought," but he maintained they are laws directing how we *ought* to think, not empirical generalizations about how we *do* think. The laws of logic are laws to which all *rational* thinking must conform and are recognized as necessary by the human understanding itself. In fact, Kant believed that the laws of thought had been discovered by the time he wrote on logic. (He died in 1804.) And he believed that the formal logic of his day was a completed science.

The final theory we shall discuss is of relatively modern origin, (4) though it has forerunners in the philosophies of Thomas Hobbes and George Berkeley. This theory is sometimes called *conventionalism*. It holds that the truths of logic are true solely by virtue of the meanings we give to words in our language. Since we can determine to use words as we will, the necessity of logical truths is a necessity *relative to the meanings we give to words*. The necessity is the result of our own determination to use words such as 'or', 'not', 'and', in the ways we do. Certain logical positivists, in the first half of this century, held a view like this. Moreover, it was maintained that since logical truths can be determined as true only by reference to the meanings of the terms employed, the way things are in the world is irrelevant to their truth or falsity. Thus, it was maintained, logical truths assert nothing about reality. We acquire our recognition of logical truths by living in a linguistic community and by reflecting on the meanings of those words that function as logical constants. The only necessity they have is the result of *our* choice to use words in certain ways. The so-called "truths" of logic, then, really assert nothing and are better regarded as rules for the use of words, not true or false statements. Since our choice is controlling, there is no grasp of necessary truth through our rational capacity, and we are free to accept whatever rules we wish.

Though conventionalism has had its day, most contemporary philosophers find it inadequate. While few will deny that logical truths are true by virtue of the meanings of the words, they want to say that *given the meanings the words do have*, the statements made *are true*. Given the ordinary meanings of 'if ___, then ___' and 'and', it surely is necessarily true that if

> If *A,* then *B*

is true, and

> *A*

is true, then

> *B*

is true.

Moreover, the suggestion that we can adopt *any* meanings we choose, and thus any principles of logic, has been especially hard to accept. In this connection, a *modified conventionalism* has been developed especially by the American logicians C. I. Lewis and Willard Van Orman Quine. Quine does not deny that logical truths depend on conventions of language for their truth, but he points out that *all* sentences have a conventional component in this respect, since we could alter all in truth-value by changing our conventions for the use of the constituent terms. In Quine's view all of our knowledge constitutes a body of sentences more or less accepted on the basis of experience. But some sentences are more central to the body than others in that they are less easily disturbed by experience than others. The truths of logic are the most stable, least easily dropped of our bundle of beliefs. We will give up or rearrange all our other beliefs if we have to before questioning laws of logic. When we discover something to which the current laws of science must attribute incompatible properties, we will seek to disprove one of the laws of science rather than discard, e.g., the law of noncontradiction. This is not to say, however, that mathematical and logical laws cannot be altered or revised. We might better deal with the various puzzles and difficulties of modern physics, for example, by changing somewhat the kind of logic we use for science. Any such change, however, is tantamount to altering our entire conceptual scheme, our entire way of looking at the world. Logical truths are, indeed, true by virtue of the meanings of the terms, so the adoption of new laws involves giving a new meaning to old terms; but the terms involved are those that organize our entire discourse about reality and, thus, our whole way of understanding reality.[29]

Quine's modified conventionalism clearly has aspects of several of the other theories and brings us back full circle to the theory of Dewey, to which it has obvious similarities. Indeed, Quine's position is sometimes referred to as *logical pragmatism*. While the truths of logic depend on the conventions of language and, thus, come to be known by reflection on language, they also organize our body of knowledge about the world and guide our scientific investigation of reality in important ways. Thus, the ultimate justification of logic is to be found in its ability to facilitate our study of reality. In *this* respect there is no fundamental difference between truths of logic and other statements; all are ultimately justifiably accepted in a body of knowledge if the system containing those statements is able to render reality intelligible. Logical truths do not *describe* reality, but, by relating statements to one another, adoption of them has consequences for the system of statements that do describe and relate more directly to the world. So the ultimate justification of logic is to be found in experience.

Despite his view that logical systems alternative to the standard ones are possible and can be taken as candidates for acceptance, Quine has not looked favorably on those that have been presented. An alternative system (sometimes called a *deviant* logic) can be thought of as a system that would reject from its list of logical truths some of those accepted in basic logic. None of the kinds of logic we have thus far discussed does this.

Systems have been proposed, however, that do not incorporate all of basic logic. None (of which this writer is aware) countenances outright contradictions, but they do not count all the standard laws among their logical truths. We shall discuss alternative logics in Chapter III.

Now, it should be clear that the answers one gives to the questions we have raised—about the source and justification of logic—depend on answers to the most central issues in all philosophy: the issues of the nature of the human mind and of reality, and the question of how we can come to have knowledge or warranted beliefs about reality. If this brief survey of some philosophical attempts to deal with the issues does no more than make this clear, it will have served a useful function.

NOTES

1. A student interested in the assessment of informal reasoning and mistakes in informal argumentative situations would profit from reading Howard Kahane, *Logic and Contemporary Rhetoric: The Use of Reason in Everyday Life* (Belmont, Calif.: Wadsworth Publshing Company, Inc., 1971).

2. There is considerable debate among logicians over whether it is *sentences* or *propositions* with which logic deals. Sentences are what one writes, prints, or utters, while propositions are what one asserts when he writes or speaks a sentence. It is argued that we can assert the same thing—state the same proposition—using different sentences (e.g., in different languages). Further discussion of this matter is to be found in Chapter III. In the present chapter the somewhat neutral term 'statement' has been employed except when it has seemed imperative to speak straightforwardly of sentences.

3. As we shall see in Chapter II, there may also be further sentences that are neither premises nor conclusions.

4. In the rest of this chapter we shall designate *arguments* by roman numerals and *argument-forms* by arabic numerals.

5. I am disregarding the special cases of conditional proofs and indirect (*reductio ad absurdum*) proofs. Such proofs introduce considerations beyond the information contained in the premises (if, indeed, there are any premises). These proof techniques are discussed in Chapter II.

6. Actually, many logicians object to these definitions for a variety of reasons. However, all would agree that if it *is* possible for the premises of an argument to be true and the conclusion false, then the argument is *not* valid. Thus, they do accept our definition as *part* of the correct definition. This is discussed further in Chapter III.

7. Though we can hardly give a satisfactory account of the meaning of "possible" in terms of what is "imaginable," in this case we can construct an obviously self-consistent story in which the premises are true and the conclusion false.

8. Actually, owing to possible equivocations in the meanings of words, what

appear to be trivial or even self-contradictory statements may, in fact, be informative, *true* statements. Consider the following: 'If I marry Jane, she will be a wife to me'. 'That lady was not a lady'.

9. For the points made in this section I am indebted to John Corcoran, "Conceptual Structure of Classical Logic," *Philosophy and Phenomenological Research*, XXXIII (September, 1972), 25–47. His distinction between "premise-conclusion" arguments and "demonstrative" arguments seems to me quite important.

10. The point really has nothing to do with the English language. The occurrence of *some* expression with that meaning is what is involved.

11. The student should be careful of the terminology. Predicates are expressions that refer to properties. Predicates are not properties. Moreover, the logician's use of the term 'predicate' is somewhat different from the grammarian's use of that term. This is discussed in Chapter II.

12. This is *not* a standard terminology. It has been adopted throughout this book and is used in at least one other, though perhaps in a more inclusive sense: Richard L. Purtill, *Logic for Philosophers* (New York: Harper & Row, 1971).

13. Actually, it is possible to dispense with symbols that name particular things. Some logicians prefer to do so for philosophical reasons. For example: W. V. Quine, *Methods of Logic*, 3d ed. (New York: Holt, Rinehart and Winston, Inc., 1972), pp. 230–234.

14. There are strong reasons for denying that identity statements assert something about two names or expressions. The statement 'The evening star is the planet Venus' is not an assertion about expressions in the English language; it says something about objects that is true regardless of how words are used in English or any other language.

15. Pioneering modern studies are those of A. N. Prior: *Time and Modality* (Oxford: Oxford University Press, 1957) and *Past, Present and Future* (Oxford: Oxford University Press, 1967). Chronological logic is discussed in Nicholas Rescher, *Topics in Philosophical Logic* (Dordrecht, Holland: D. Reidel Publishing Company, 1968). This is a topic for advanced students.

16. Actually, owing to an ingenious proof by Kurt Gödel, we know that there cannot be a system of logic in which every mathematical truth can be derived.

17. Some of the difficulties of higher-order logic are discussed in W. V. Quine, *Philosophy of Logic,* Foundations of Philosophy Series (Englewood Cliffs, N.J.: Prentice-Hall, Inc., 1970), pp. 66–68, and in William Kneale and Martha Kneale, *The Development of Logic* (Oxford: Oxford University Press, 1962), pp. 621–626. These discussions are meant for advanced students, however.

18. Because of its origin, syllogistic logic is sometimes referred to as "Aristotelian logic." This is misleading, since the usual ways of presenting it differ in important ways from Aristotle's presentation.

19. Actually, there is a further limitation to traditional logic: it is limited to categorical statements assumed to have "existential import"; i.e., the constituent terms are assumed to apply to existing objects, so that, for example, if 'men' is a term, it is assumed that there are some men.

20. Assuming that for every property or characterizing term, there is a corresponding set of things having that property or to which the term applies, leads to contradictions. Moreover, in speaking of objects and their properties,

some logicians believe we need not assume the existence of abstract "objects" such as set, whereas set theory does involve the existence of sets.

21. Again, the advanced student will find an argument for this conclusion in the books given in note 17, as follows: Quine, pp. 64–72; Kneale and Kneale, 737–742. The Kneales also maintain that identity is not a concept of logic.

22. This may sound strange because, intuitively, a denial of a statement amounts to asserting the opposite of that statement. If one considers randomly selected logical truths and falsehoods, there may be no obvious sense in which they assert the opposite of one another. The surprise should be allayed somewhat if we notice that logical truths and falsehoods are strange kinds of statements to begin with, and it is not clear they assert anything at all. Moreover, we can, if we choose, regard the above definition as *one* possible interpretation of denial, among others.

23. A deductive system for propositional logic *can* be developed that can be reduced to mechanical rules and thus can be made into a decision-procedure. The procedure is extremely cumbersome, however.

24. This is not to say we *could not* swallow the pill. See the theory of Quine outlined toward the end of this section.

25. Different things are sometimes meant by the phrase "laws of logic" in this context: (1) logically true sentences, (2) metalogical statements that assert that all statements of a certain form are logically true, (3) rules of inference. It will do no harm to accept all three, in our present discussion, as "laws of logic."

26. Dewey's views are developed in John Dewey, *Logic: The Theory of Inquiry* (New York: Holt, Rinehart and Winston, Inc., 1938).

27. 'Platonism' is also used by some writers for a theory about the nature of mathematical and logical "objects" such as sets. Necessarily, our present discussion fails to bring out various forms these theories have taken. We have, for example, described only one kind of realist view. A good introduction to these issues is Stephen F. Barker, *Philosophy of Mathematics,* Foundations of Philosophy Series (Englewood Cliffs, N.J.: Prentice-Hall, Inc., 1964), Chap. IV.

28. Realists and some advocates of psychologism are historically distinguished by their attitudes toward mathematical "objects" and other abstract entities. Realists held those to exist independently of the mind; thus, the laws of logic and mathematics describe reality. An alternative theory, usually called "conceptualism," regards such objects as creations of the mind, existing only as ideas in the mind. A further theory proposed by some philosophers of mathematics holds that logic and mathematics are not about an independent reality at all. The laws and theorems of mathematics are simply useful sets of symbols and rules for their manipulation. They are intellectual games with important applications. If logic and mathematics have a subject-matter, it is the formal characteristics of certain symbols and symbol systems. These theorists are called "formalists." Formalist theories raise important questions about infinity in mathematics.

29. Quine's views are conveniently outlined in his introduction to *Methods of Logic* and are given in greater detail in *Philosophy of Logic.*

II

Alternative Approaches within Logic

1. ARTIFICIAL AND NATURAL LANGUAGES

In an earlier section we discussed in very general terms the idea of a logical system; we indicated that a variety of logical techniques have been devised for testing arguments for validity (and statements for logical truth). It will be useful to the student to be aware of some of these alternatives in somewhat greater detail. Not only will this facilitate the ability to read and understand different logic books; it will also give a better understanding of some central aims and goals of logicians.

At the very outset we should discuss two different understandings of the symbolism employed in logic. Beginning logic texts sometimes utilize one or the other approach, and students are rarely aware that there is an alternative. First, the logician may proceed as if constructing a kind of special language with its own precise rules. He or she will specify an alphabet, possible acceptable combinations among the symbols that constitute the alphabet, and what counts as a "sentence" in the language. The logical system that is developed and the techniques employed are designed for sentences and "arguments" in that language. These procedures are made applicable to arguments in some ordinary language through the possibility of "translation" of arguments in the "natural" language into the symbolism of the artificial language. So long as the translation meets certain conditions, it will be the case that if the symbolized argument is valid, so is the argument in the natural language.

A somewhat more common way of treating the symbolism is to regard it as abbreviating expressions of the natural language directly. Thus, a logician might say: Let '*P*' be the sentence 'Mary ate a hot dog'. Here, the letter '*P*' is not a symbol of a special "language," it is a shorthand way of writing the sentence 'Mary ate a hot dog'. We might stipulate ahead of time that we shall use upper-case letters of English, beginning with '*P*' and running through '*Z*' to abbreviate whole sentences in English, and, if we need more letters, add a subscript numeral to the letters already in use. We would then have infinitely many letters to be used to abbreviate sentences; each of the following, for example, could be used: 'P_1', 'R_{32}', 'T_2', and so on. Notice the savings obtained with respect to the following arguments I and II, one a partial symbolization of the other:

I

Either Mary ate a hot dog or Mary ate a hamburger,
or she ate a hot dog *and* she ate a hamburger.
Mary did not eat a hot dog.
Therefore, Mary ate a hamburger.

II

Either *P* or *Q*, or *P* and *Q*.
It is not the case that *P*.
Therefore, *Q*.

Moreover, further economy is to be obtained if we can abbreviate the logical constants contained in these arguments. One such set of abbreviations often employed is as follows: [1]

'either *P* or *Q* (or both)'	by	'$(P \lor Q)$'
'either *P* or *Q* (but *not* both)'	by	'$(P \underline{\lor} Q)$'
'if *P*, then *Q*'	by	'$(P \supset Q)$'
'P and Q'	by	'$(P \& Q)$'
'it is not the case that *P*'	by	'$-P$'
'P, if and only if Q'	by	'$(P \equiv Q)$'

It is important to note that each dyadic logical constant, or "connective," comes with two parentheses. These help keep clear what is being said in contexts where the *grouping* of sentences might be important. If we let '*P*' abbreviate 'Mary ate a hot dog', and let '*Q*' abbreviate 'Mary ate a hamburger', consider the differences between the following: $-(P \& Q)$; $(-P \& Q)$. Using these abbreviations, our argument I becomes:

III

$(P \lor Q)$
$-P$
Q

Now, the student first learning symbolic logic need not be overly concerned with the distinction between these two approaches to the symbolism. In a logic course, the student most likely will be working with a symbolism similar to that in other logic courses and doing much the same thing with it. When dealing with arguments in ordinary language, the student will be seeking an appropriate symbolic "translation" on the one hand or an appropriate symbolic "abbreviation" on the other. The processes are so very similar they are often referred to indiscriminately as "symbolizing" arguments.

There are, however, pedagogical and theoretical advantages and disadvantages to both presentations. As an artificial language is a prerequisite to the axiomatic presentation of a logical system, we can bring out some of these advantages and disadvantages in our discussion of the two main kinds of logical systems.

There is a further use of the symbolism of logic aside from that of abbreviating particular statements and symbols of the natural language. The logician sometimes uses his symbolism to talk in a general way about sentences or arguments of the natural language that have a certain *form*. He might say, e.g.: "Let *P* and *Q* be any sentences at all; then any argument of the following form is deductively valid:

$(P \lor Q)$
$-P$
Therefore, *Q*."

Here, the letters do not stand for particular statements, and the expression '$(P \lor Q)$' is not a shorthand way of asserting a sentence. Rather, it is a *sentence-form*. If we disregard the parentheses, we *get* a sentence from '$(P \lor Q)$' by *replacing* '*P*' with a sentence, '$\lor$' by 'or', and '*Q*' by a sentence. It is very convenient to have symbolic means of talking about the forms of sentences and arguments. It is also important to keep clear when we are using symbols as abbreviations for English expressions and when we are using them to display the forms of sentences and arguments. The best way to do this is to have different symbols for each use. Various devices are employed for doing this. In the rest of our discussion, '*P*' through '*Z*' are reserved for the abbreviatory function, '*A*' through '*O*' for the other.[2]

We should notice that a *sentence-form* asserts nothing and is not true or false. It "represents," in some sense, the structure of many sentences, each of which is a result of making appropriate replacements in the sentence-form. If we let '*P*' be an abbreviation of the sentence 'Mary ate a hot dog', and '*Q*' be the sentence 'Mary ate a hamburger', then '$(P \lor Q)$' *is* a sentence that can be true or false; but '$(A \lor B)$' is *not* a sentence; it is a form that displays the structure of the sentence '$(P \lor Q)$'. We make the sentence-form '$(A \lor B)$' a sentence either by replacing the letters with symbols that abbreviate sentences of the natural language or by replacing them with sentences of the natural language, depending on whether or not we are using an artificial language.

A further point concerning the symbolism must be discussed briefly. We have taken the symbols for the logical constants to be abbreviations for English expressions. This is somewhat misleading, insofar as the English expressions do not always have the precise meanings that the logician wants to assign to the symbolic logical constants. These differences create "translation" problems, which we shall take up in Chapter III. The usual way in which the logician guarantees the precise meanings of his symbolic logical constants is to state at the outset the conditions under which sentences containing them are true or false. This is usually done by means of truth-tables. Such tables for the constants we have chosen might appear as follows:

A	$-A$
T	F
F	T

A	B	$(A \lor B)$	$(A \underline{\lor} B)$	$(A \supset B)$	$(A \,\&\, B)$	$(A \equiv B)$
T	T	T	F	T	T	T
T	F	T	T	F	F	F
F	T	T	T	T	F	F
F	F	F	F	T	F	T

Several things should be noted. These tables provide what are called *contextual definitions* of the logical constants. This means that they are defined in the context of a sentence or sentence-form in which they occur. Second, the definition for each constant is very general. The information contained in the column for '$(A \lor B)$' is that any sentence of that form is true if at least one of the constituent sentences is true. Third, a very complex sentence can have that form. For example, the sentence '$((P \supset Q) \lor (R \,\&\, S))$' has that form. The table tells us that this sentence is true if either '$(P \supset Q)$' is true, or '$(R \,\&\, S)$' is true, or if both are true. We must next apply the definitions for '$\supset$' and for '&' to discover the further truth-conditions of the larger sentence. Oddly enough, the large sentence is true if 'P' is false. The table for '$\supset$' shows that if 'P' is false, then '$(P \supset Q)$' is true, in which case '$((P \supset Q) \lor (R \,\&\, S))$' is true. This fact leads up to the last point we shall make in this section. '$(P \supset Q)$' is taken as an abbreviation for an English sentence of the form 'If ___, then ___'. We do not usually regard such a sentence as true *merely* because the 'If ___' clause is false. This is part of the "translation" problem we are leaving for Chapter III.

2. NATURAL DEDUCTION SYSTEMS

We are all familiar with deduction. Detectives on television sometimes perform amazing feats of deduction that leave us greatly impressed with the potential powers of human reason. The fact is that we all engage in deduction regularly; an important part of reasoning involves deducing conclusions from information we possess. However, it is rare for reasoning to consist solely of an argument in the special sense of the term we have adopted. Normally, we do not simply state our premises and directly infer the conclusion; it is more common to reason from the premises to further statements, which are then used to deduce the conclusion we want. Our reasoning consists in a chain of inferences that lead up to our final conclusion. Moreover, we sometimes make additional assumptions "for the purpose of the argument," asking ourselves what would be the case if the assumption were true or false. Thus, not all of the statements employed in the deduction are taken as true or known to be true at the outset. Nor are all of them premises.

Deduction is obviously a useful tool if we have some knowledge and want to *discover* what follows from that knowledge. We want to see what conclusion or conclusions that information "leads to." In such a case we do not have an "argument" the validity of which is in question; we want to *get* conclusions from our premises. Deduction is also useful as a *justificatory* tool. We can show that a certain conclusion is justified on the basis of given data if we can show that the conclusion can be deduced from the statements expressing that data.

Let us examine a sample case of a deduction. A purely imaginary student might be faced with a crucial choice during final exam week. He has two exams remaining—in logic and history—neither of which he has studied for. He does not have time to study for both. He also knows special further facts about his situation that can help him determine which, if either, course he will study for. We can arrange his information in the form of a list:

(1) If I do not study for history, I shall study for logic.
(2) I shall study for history if the library has the book I need, and I can get to the library before it closes; otherwise, I shall not study for history.
(3) If I eat lunch, I shall not get to the library before it closes.
(4) I am hungry, and so I shall eat lunch.

Now, he might very well see immediately that, given these facts, he will study for logic. But, if he happens not to see it (after all, he *is* in the midst of final exams), he might deduce that fact in the following way:

Since, according to (4), I shall eat lunch, and (3) says that if I eat lunch, I won't make it to the library on time, it follows that:

(5)   I won't get to the library before it closes.

But, (2) says that if it is not the case both that I get to the library in time and it has the book I need, then I shall not study for history. So, because (2) and (5) are true, it follows that:

(6)   I won't study for history.

Well, (1) says that if I don't study for history, then I'll study for logic, so

(7)   I shall study for logic.

Let us notice some features of this "deduction." We arrived at the conclusion by a series or chain of inferences from the information we had. Moreover, we could cite the prior sentences on which we relied in deducing each conclusion. If we rewrote the entire deduction as a long "argument," then each sentence would be either an initial "premise" or derived from one or more premises, or from a sentence itself derived ultimately from the premises. Something else is involved in our deduction, however. Each time we "derived" a sentence from others, we implicitly were accepting the argument consisting of the premises used and conclusion deduced as valid. For example, at one point, our imaginary reasoner concluded that he would not get to the library in time. Implicitly, he was accepting the following argument as valid:

III

If I eat lunch, then I shall not get to the library before it closes.
I shall eat lunch.
Therefore, I shall not get to the library before it closes.

In the last chapter we saw that the validity of an argument depends on its form. So, accepting the argument above as valid amounts to accepting it as having a valid argument-form. We can explain the notion of a valid argument-form in propositional logic as follows. First, we shall use our symbols for representing argument-forms. Appearing in argument-forms, then, are sentence-forms—i.e., expressions which, when replaced with other appropriate expressions, become sentences. We need next to define the notion of a *standard* or *uniform substitution* in an argument-form of propositional logic. We make a standard substitution if (a) we replace every letter in the form with a sentence, (b) the *same* sentence replaces *every* occurrence of that letter, and (c) no *other* replacement is made. Any argument that is the result of a standard substitution in an argument-form is a *standard substitution-instance* of that form. Now, we can say that *an argument-form is valid* if, and only if, every standard substitution-instance of it is valid. Let us consider the subargument labeled "III" above. That argument clearly is a standard substitution-instance of the following form (represented in two equivalent ways):

IV	V
If A, then B.	$(A \supset B)$
A.	A
Therefore, B.	B

Involved in our longer deduction, then, was our acceptance of this argument-form as valid. In accepting it as such, we have implicitly accepted what we earlier called a "rule of inference"—a rule to the effect that from sentences of the form *(A ⊃ B)* and *A,* we can infer *B.* If that is indeed a truth-preserving rule, then any argument that is a standard substitution-instance of the displayed form is valid. That this *is* a valid argument-form is obvious, and no one would have serious doubts about accepting the corresponding rule of inference.

Deduction, we have seen, utilizes rules of inference, by which we justify the steps in a deduction. Moreover, we have seen one way of arriving at or discovering a rule of inference: we discover an obviously valid argument-form and adopt the rule that any argument that is a standard substitution-instance of it is valid—i.e., the rule that we can deduce the conclusion of such an argument from the premises. Clearly, it would be an important piece of logical knowledge to systematically collect the principal rules of inference employed in deduction. Systems of natural deduction partially serve this function. They consist of a set of rules of inference by which deductions may be constructed. Normally, the rules chosen either are obviously acceptable ones employed naturally in our reasoning or else can be readily justified, given the purposes for which rules of inference are wanted. Because the technique of deduction proceeds in a way like everyday reasoning, and since such systems commonly employ readily recognized principles, such a system is called a "natural deduction" system. It is also customary for such a system to specify a standard manner of writing out a deduction, in which it is made clear on what basis each line or step in the deduction is made. A deduction made according to the rules of such a system is sometimes called a *proof of the conclusion from the premises* or, alternatively, a *derivation* of the conclusion from the premises. The result is a logical system that can be used for a variety of purposes. Using it, we can take given premises and deduce conclusions that validly follow from them, or we can take a given argument and *show* that it is valid *by* deducing the conclusion from the premises.

In the remainder of this section on natural deduction we shall outline the chief kinds of rules that occur in these systems and shall illustrate their applications.

a. Valid Inference Forms

The first step in developing a natural deduction system is to indicate the valid argument-forms that are to be utilized as rules of inference. We shall give a list of valid inference patterns and then explain how they are applied. The list is quite large in order to familiarize the reader with a large number of such rules. A solid line is drawn in each case to separate the premises from the conclusion and also to do the work of the English expression 'therefore'. A commonly accepted name for each pattern is given along with a commonly used abbreviation for the name:

(1) $(A \supset B)$
$$\frac{A}{B}$$ Modus Ponens (M.P.)

(2) $(A \supset B)$
$$\frac{-B}{-A}$$ Modus Tollens (M.T.)

(3) $\dfrac{A \& B}{A} \quad \dfrac{A \& B}{B}$
Simplification (Simp.)

(4) A
B
$$\overline{(A \& B)}$$ Conjunction (Conj.)

(5) $\dfrac{A}{(A \lor B)} \quad \dfrac{A}{(B \lor A)}$
Addition (Add.)

(6) $(A \supset B)$ Hypothetical Syllogism
$(B \supset C)$ (Hyp.)
$$\overline{(A \supset C)}$$ also:
Chain Argument

(7) $\dfrac{(A \lor B)}{-A} \quad \dfrac{(A \lor B)}{-B}$
$$\dfrac{}{B} \qquad \dfrac{}{A}$$
Disjunctive Syllogism (Dis.)
also:
Disjunctive Argument

(8) $\dfrac{-(A \& B)}{A} \quad \dfrac{-(A \& B)}{B}$
$$\dfrac{}{-B} \qquad \dfrac{}{-A}$$
Conjunctive Argument (C.A.)

(9) $(A \supset B)$ Simple Constructive
$(C \supset B)$ Dilemma (S.C.D.)
$$\frac{(A \lor C)}{B}$$

(10) $(A \supset B)$ Complex Constructive
$(C \supset D)$ Dilemma (C.C.D.)
$$\frac{(A \lor C)}{(B \lor D)}$$

(11) $(A \supset B)$ Simple Destructive
$(A \supset C)$ Dilemma (S.D.D.)
$$\frac{(-B \lor -C)}{-A}$$

(12) $(A \supset B)$ Complex Destructive
$(C \supset D)$ Dilemma (C.D.D.)
$$\frac{(-B \lor -D)}{(-A \lor -C)}$$

(13) $$\frac{(A \supset B)}{(A \supset (A \& B))}$$ Absorption (Abs.)

These argument-forms are utilized in the following way.[3] The premises of the argument at hand are symbolized. We then seek to make a series of deductions from the premises until we arrive at the symbolized conclusion of the argument. Each deductive step is, in fact, an argument within the larger argument; each step consists in inferring a conclusion from sentences that occur before it. Of course, at the outset we have only the premises. From these we deduce conclusions, which can be used as premises in new subarguments to establish further conclusions. This process is continued until the final conclusion is reached (of course, this will happen only if the argument is valid). Each subargument employed must be justified by reference to the list of valid argument-forms. This means that we must be able to show that the argument is a standard substitution-instance of one of the listed argument-forms.

The process is best understood through an example. Suppose a member of Congress were to explain to a colleague why he or she is depressed:

> Either we must cut the budget or we shall create greater inflation. If we must cut the budget, then we shall cut the military appropriation. If we create greater inflation, we shall not be reelected. But we must keep the country first in armaments, so we shall not cut the military appropriation. Therefore, we shall not cut the budget and shall not be reelected.

We could test this reasoning as follows:

Symbolic dictionary	P: We must cut the budget.
	Q: We shall create greater inflation.
	R: We shall cut the military appropriation.
	S: We shall be reelected.
	T: We must keep the country first in armaments.

Argument		
	1. $(P \lor Q)$	Premise
	2. $(P \supset R)$	Premise
	3. $(Q \supset -S)$	Premise
	4. $(T \,\&\, -R)$	Premise
	5. $-R$	4 Simp.
	6. $-P$	2, 5 M.T.
	7. Q	1, 6 Dis.
	8. $-S$	3, 7 M.P.
	9. $(-P \,\&\, -S)$	6, 8 Conj.

The deduction has been written out in such a way that the justification of each step is indicated to the right of the conclusion drawn at that step. The step is justified if the argument having as premise(s) the line(s) cited and as conclusion the new line is a standard substitution-instance of the argument-form cited. Line 5, for example, is the conclusion of an argument that has line 4 as its premise. That argument is a standard substitution-instance of one of the two patterns labeled *Simplification.* We can then go on to use line 5 as a premise, if we need it, in a further subargument. In fact, line 5 is utilized in obtaining line 6.

Strictly speaking, the information on the right—the justifications—is not part of the argument. Putting it in is good practice, however, as it makes proofs easier to follow and easier to check. Checking *is* important, as care must be taken in applying the definition of substitution-instance. For example, students often mistakenly think that each of the following is a correct application of *Modus Ponens:*

$$(--P \supset Q) \qquad (P \supset Q)$$
$$\underline{P} \qquad\qquad\quad \underline{Q}$$
$$Q \text{ (Wrong)} \qquad\quad P \text{ (Wrong)}$$

The inference on the right is so common a pattern, it has a name: the *fallacy of affirming the consequent.* The inference on the left is instructive because it is, in fact, deductively valid. It is not, however, a standard-substitution instance of *Modus Ponens* or of any other argument-form in our list. This shows that the list is not sufficient for demonstrating the validity of every valid propositional argument; the list must be supplemented. We usually do so by adding a somewhat different kind of rule, known as a rule of *replacement* or *equivalence.*

b. Rule of Replacement

The need for the rule of replacement is clear in the argument above. It is clear that '*P*' and '*− −P*' are equivalent. In fact, these sentences are *logically equivalent;* whatever true-value the one has, so does the other.[4] This means that any sentence of which '*P*' is a part will retain *its* truth-value if '*− −P*' is put in place of '*P*'. Of course, if we make the replacement, we get a *new* sentence. But the new compound sentence will have the same truth-value as the old one. Thus, the original sentence implies the new one, since it is not possible for the old sentence to be true and the new one false. Thus, we are safe in deducing the new sentence from the old one. The rule of replacement tells us, essentially, that we may deduce from a sentence another that is just like it, except that where the first contains a given sentence, *A,* the second contains a sentence, *B,* that is logically equivalent to *A.*

A great many pairs of sentences are logically equivalent. It is customary to combine the rule of replacement with a list of well-recognized and widely used pairs of equivalent sentences. When this is done, replacement is limited to cases where the sentences being exchanged are substitution-instances of pairs in the list. We shall formulate the rule of replacement in this way:

> *Rule of Replacement:* If ϕ occurs as a line of a proof, then ψ may be written as a line if: (a) ψ is exactly like ϕ except that ϕ contains A and ψ contains B in place of A, and (b) $(A \equiv B)$ or $(B \equiv A)$ is a substitution-instance of one of the following logically true sentence-forms: [5]

(1) $((A) \equiv (A \,\&\, A))$ Tautology
      $((A) \equiv (A \lor \overline{A}))$ (Taut.)

(2) $((A \supset B) \equiv (-A \lor B))$
      $((A \supset B) \equiv -(A \,\&\, -B))$
      $((A \lor B) \equiv (-A \supset B))$
      $((A \lor B) \equiv -(-A \,\&\, -B))$ Change of Connective
      $((A \,\&\, B) \equiv -(A \supset -B))$ (C.C.)
      $((A \,\&\, B) \equiv -(-A \lor -B))$
      $((A \equiv B) \equiv ((A \supset B) \,\&\, (B \supset A)))$

(3) $((A \supset B) \equiv (-B \supset -A))$ Contraposition (Cont.)
                                also:
                            Transposition (Trans.)

(4) $(A \equiv --A)$ Double Negation (D.N.)

(5) $((A \,\&\, B) \equiv (B \,\&\, A))$ Commutativity (Com.)
      $((A \lor B) \equiv (B \lor A))$

(6) $(-(A \,\&\, B) \equiv (-A \lor -B))$ De Morgan's Laws (D.M.)
      $(-(A \lor B) \equiv (-A \,\&\, -B))$

(7) $((A \,\&\, (B \,\&\, C)) \equiv ((A \,\&\, B) \,\&\, C))$ Associativity (Assoc.)
      $((A \lor (B \lor C)) \equiv ((A \lor B) \lor C))$

(8) $((A \,\&\, (B \lor C)) \equiv ((A \,\&\, B) \lor (A \,\&\, C)))$ Distribution (Dist.)
      $((A \lor (B \,\&\, C)) \equiv ((A \lor B) \,\&\, (A \lor C)))$

(9) $(((A \,\&\, B) \supset C) \equiv ((A \supset (B \supset C)))$ Exportation (Exp.)

The utility of the rule of replacement consists in the fact that it permits making replacements *within* a sentence, as well as replacing an entire sentence by another. In this respect, applications of this rule can differ radically from applications of the valid argument-forms, since they are not to be applied within a line. Thus, the following would be mistaken:

(1) $((P \,\&\, Q) \supset R)$ Premise
(2) P Premise
(3) $(P \supset R)$ 1 Simp. WRONG
(4) R 3, 2 M.P.

While applications of the valid forms within a line do not always create trouble, this example shows that they can lead to errors. The rule of replacement, however, *does* sanction applications within a line:

(1)	$(--P \supset Q)$	Premise
(2)	P	Premise
(3)	$(P \supset Q)$	1, D.N.
(4)	Q	3, 2 M.P.

The set of rules we have given is complete for propositional logic in the sense that any argument that is valid in propositional logic can be shown valid using the rules. We have not given instructions for applying the rules that will guarantee that we will always come up with the proof of a valid argument. Constructing proofs is still a matter of cleverness and luck. It is actually better for beginners not to have such instructions. In the first place, they are very complicated. But, also, the beginner can better learn important rules of inference and important logical equivalences by having to work out deductions on his or her own.

The rules given are, in a sense, *more* than complete. By this it is meant that we could eliminate some rules and still have a set sufficient for every proof in propositional logic. We can show that a rule can be eliminated if we can indicate how any proof using it could be accomplished without that rule. If this can be done, the rule is said to be *derived* from the others. *Modus tollens* can be derived from the others in our list. It has the form:

$$(A \supset B)$$
$$\underline{-B}$$
$$-A$$

Any argument of that form can be done as follows:

(1)	$(A \supset B)$	Premise
(2)	$-B$	Premise
(3)	$(-B \supset -A)$	1 Cont.
(4)	$-A$	3, 2 M.P.

Derived rules are often added to a system for the obvious reason that they shorten proofs. We shall turn to two further kinds of rules that shorten proofs and that have important applications. Most natural deduction systems utilize them in one form or another.

c. Conditional Proof

The technique of conditional proof is employed in everyday argumentation as well as in logic texts. We can show this with a sample argument. Let us again suppose a congressional representative to be discussing an upcoming vote with a colleague. They agree on this much:

> If we cut the military appropriation, then: we shall cut the budget and we shall not create greater inflation. And, if we do not create greater inflation, then we shall be reelected.

If it were not already obvious to his or her colleague, the representative could easily show that if they cut the military appropriation, they will be reelected:

> Suppose we *do* cut the military appropriation. Then we shall cut the budget and shall not create greater inflation. But, since we won't create greater inflation, we shall be reelected. So, if we cut the military appropriation, we shall be reelected.

The crucial step here is that we *suppose* something is the case in addition to the premises. From the premises and additional assumption we derive a conclusion. From that we conclude that if the premises are true, then if the assumption is true, so is the derived conclusion. In other words, if the premises are true, so is a certain conditional statement—viz., a conditional with the assumption as antecedent and the derived conclusion as consequent. The proof shows that the original premises imply that conditional sentence, since it is not possible for the premises to be true and the conditional false.[6]

Such a proof introduces something new into the proof techniques: we can now enter a line that is neither a premise nor logically implied by the premises. In writing proofs, we must clearly indicate and keep track of assumptions, so that we draw no final conclusions that depend on the assumption. We have introduced the assumption conditionally; i.e., we are interested in what *would* be the case *if* it were true. We have not literally assumed it *is* true. Thus, any conclusion drawn using it can be taken as established *only* if the supposition and the premises are true. In the deduction, then, we must keep a record of which lines logically depend on the supposition. The final conclusion—the conditional sentence itself—does not depend on the assumption, since it says (in effect) that if the assumption is true, then so is the derived conclusion. *That* statement depends only on the premises. Once having written the conditional statement, we are no longer supposing anything, for we have *shown* that *if* the antecedent is true, so is the consequent.

To keep track of the lines on which sentences in a conditional proof depend, various techniques have been devised. One common technique can be illustrated by symbolizing the sample argument and using Conditional Proof (C.P.):

(1)	$(R \supset (P \& -Q))$		Premise
(2)	$(-Q \supset S)$		Premise
→(3)	R		Assumption
(4)	$(P \& -Q)$		1, 3 M.P.
(5)	$-Q$		4 Simp.
(6)	S		2, 5 M.P.
(7)	$(R \supset S)$		3–6 C.P.

Here, the arrow points to the assumption that was made; the line under line 6 indicates that the sequence of sentences 3–6 all depend on the assumption, together with the premises. The conclusion, line 7, does *not* depend on the assumption; if the premises are true, so is line 7, and the sequence 3–6 shows this. Once the line has been drawn, of course, we have "dismissed" the assumption, so neither it nor anything dependent on it may be utilized again unless independently demonstrated (or assumed). This is important, as we sometimes use C.P. to establish a conditional sentence *within* a proof, as a step in getting some further conclusion. Obviously, we do not want any further lines to depend on the assumption.

We shall turn to another mode of argumentation that employs assumptions made "for the sake of the argument."

d. Indirect Proof

Not all rules of inference are derived from valid argument-forms, as we have seen; indeed, those that can be obtained in that way often are not presented to the student in that fashion. All that is absolutely requisite in a rule of inference is that it be truth-preserving—i.e., that it should never permit us to deduce a false conclusion from premises all of which are true. Rules can be justified, then, if we can show they are truth-preserving whether or not they refer to valid argument-forms.

An important kind of rule of inference, often employed in natural deduction systems, is sometimes called the rule of *indirect proof* or *re-*

ductio ad absurdum. In ordinary reasoning a technique like it is often employed.

According to our characterization of a valid argument, it is not possible for the premises to be true and the conclusion false. That is, if the premises are all true, so is the conclusion. Now, whenever the conclusion is true, a denial of it must be false. So, we can recharacterize validity as follows: an argument is valid if, and only if, it is not possible for the premises to all be true and a denial of the conclusion to be true also. The method of indirect proof capitalizes on this fact. It amounts to showing that it cannot be the case that the premises and a denial of the conclusion are all true. This is done in the following manner. We add an additional assumption to the argument—a denial of the conclusion. We then show that the resulting argument leads to a contradiction. Since no contradictory sentence can be true, it follows that not all of the sentences utilized in the proof can possibly be true. In particular, it follows that it is not possible for the premises of the original argument to all be true and a denial of the conclusion to be true also. *If* all the premises are true, a *denial* of the conclusion *must* be false. So, if the premises are all true, the *conclusion* must be true.

In everyday reasoning we sometimes resort to this pattern of argument. We say: "What if the conclusion were false?" We then show that assuming its denial true yields absurd results. We then conclude that the conclusion must be true if the premises are true. A brief example can illustrate the method well. We can easily show that there is no even prime number greater than two by an indirect argument:

> A prime number is any number divisible without remainder *only* by itself and 1. An even number is any number divisible without remainder by 2. Now, suppose there *is* a prime number that is even and greater than two. Then, it is divisible only by itself and 1. But, since it is even, it is divisible by 2. Now, since it is greater than 2, it is divisible by 2, by itself, and by 1. But that contradicts our earlier conclusion that it is divisible *only* by itself and 1. So, there cannot be such a number.

Indirect proof illustrates a technique of reasoning with important applications.[7] It is a method that permits us to assume certain propositions "for the purpose of the argument." We can show the consequences of such an assumption and then draw a further conclusion based on the result. (In fact, it can be shown that any proof done by the indirect-proof method can be done instead using conditional proof and the other rules.)

The rules of derivation that permit taking on additional assumptions allow us to extend the application of our natural deduction systems in an important way. So far, we have described such systems as enabling us to derive conclusions from given premises. By permitting taking on assumptions, the technique can be employed to show that logically true propositions *are* logically true. The method of indirect proof is especially suited to this task (though it is not the *only* method available for this purpose). In effect, we assume a denial of the statement is true. We then show that this leads to a contradiction; thus, the assumption cannot be true. But, if the assumption cannot be true, then the statement of which it is a denial *must* be true. A statement that *must* be true is a logical truth.

A natural deduction system, then, can be employed not only for deriving or proving conclusions from premises, but also for proving logical truths. Logicians often describe the latter procedure as "deriving a sentence from no premises." This misleadingly suggests that one gives an argument with no premises. Though a sense can be given this description, it is better to say that an argument is given that shows that the truth of the sentence depends on no premises. A sentence that is logically true is true no matter what else is true. By showing it is logically true, we show that it must be true independently of any other sentences.

We shall give a proof of a logical truth, using the method of indirect proof, and then display another proof of the same sentence using conditional proof.

To prove: $(P \supset (-Q \lor P))$

(1)	$-(P \supset (-Q \lor P))$	Assumption for I.P.
(2)	$-(-P \lor (-Q \lor P))$	1 C.C.
(3)	$(--P \& -(-Q \lor P))$	2 D.M.
(4)	$--P$	3 Simp.
(5)	P	4 D.N.
(6)	$-(-Q \lor P)$	3 Simp.
(7)	$(--Q \& -P)$	6 D.M.
(8)	$-P$	7 Simp.
(9)	$P \& -P$	5, 8 Conj.
(10)	$(P \supset (-Q \lor P))$	1–9 I.P.

To prove: $(P \supset (-Q \lor P))$

(1)	P	Assumption for C.P.
(2)	$P \lor -Q$	1 Add.
(3)	$-Q \lor P$	2 Com.
(4)	$(P \supset (-Q \lor P))$	1–3 C.P.

Though most of the principles of natural deduction have been known for some time, the systematic formulation and presentation of *systems* of deduction in this form is of relatively recent origin in logic. This has been due, in large measure, to the fact that modern logic developed along with important work in mathematics. A method referred to as "axiomatization" has been especially fruitful in mathematics and geometry, and this approach has been widely employed in logic also. We shall now turn to a discussion of its primary features.

3. AXIOMATIC DEDUCTIVE SYSTEMS

Most students of logic are somewhat familiar with the axiomatic presentation of a body of knowledge from the high school study of geometry. Such a presentation begins with certain basic undefined terms, which are used to define others. Then a list is given of certain basic sentences called "axioms" and "postulates." (The modern practice is to make no distinction among axioms and postulates; all basic sentences of the system are called axioms.) From the basic sentences (e.g., "the whole is greater than its parts") further sentences are deduced, called *theorems.* Any theorems proved to follow from the axioms may be employed in deducing further theorems. In this way, a body of theorems of geometry can be deductively established.

Let us note important features of such a deductive system. First, the concepts employed consist of two kinds—the basic ones used to define the others (called *primitive* or *undefined* terms), and the defined terms. If the basic terms employed are relatively well understood, a kind of conceptual clarity is achieved, since all other terms are defined by the basic ones. In any event, the clarity of the conceptual apparatus reduces to grasping the basic terms. Of course, it is not possible to define *every* concept used in the system without being involved in an infinite process of definition, or in circularity. To define a term, one must use other terms. Aside from an infinite process, the only way we could define all the terms used would be to define some by means of others, and then turn around and define those others by means of the original terms. All terms *would* be defined, but in a circular fashion so that no greater clarity would be achieved.

In addition to basic terms, the system uses basic sentences. These were taken in the traditional Euclidean geometry to be self-evident true statements of geometry, all phrased using either the primitive or defined terms of the system. Since all theorems are logically deduced from the axioms, the set of theorems deduced, along with the axioms, will constitute a body of knowledge about geometry. Such a procedure *organizes* a body of knowledge in several important respects. The most basic concepts are indicated at the outset, and those statements upon which the subject-matter can be based are picked out and utilized in arriving at further truths. Displayed at the outset are a set of concepts and assumptions sufficient for that subject-matter; the subject-matter is presented as a development from the basis. Large parts of mathematics have been formulated in this fashion, and there have been various suggestions for organizing portions of other sciences in this way.[8] Moreover, there may be several sets of concepts that can be used to define the others, and alternative sets of sentences that can serve as axioms. Thus, a given subject-matter may permit quite different axiom systems, each of which yields the same set of theorems in the end.

When a body of knowledge, such as geometry, is presented and developed as an axiom system, the basic principles of logic together with the principles of identity are normally taken for granted. Standard basic logic with identity is said to "underlie" the system or be "the underlying logic." Is it possible to organize *logical* knowledge in this way—as an axiom system? The answer is "yes," and, in fact, axiomatic presentations have been more common historically than natural deduction systems. Most such presentations, however, appear much different from most presentations of natural deduction systems. The vast difference in appearance, however, is due more to requirements imposed by the different purposes for which the systems are wanted than to basic and necessary differences between the methods. It *is* necessary that a formal, artificial language be specified for a fully axiomatized system, while most textbooks present natural deduction in a more informal manner. This, however, is for pedagogical reasons, since some books *do* present natural deduction for a formalized language.

The student may well wonder what could serve as a basis for axiomatic logic; i.e., what *are* basic "truths" of logic that could serve as axioms? One answer is that a proposition is a truth of logic if it can be determined as true using only logic. And, of course, we have already called attention to such truths and called them "logical truths." For example, using the symbolism earlier employed, any proposition having one of the following forms is a logical truth:

$$-(A \,\&\, -A), \quad (A \lor -A), \quad (((A \supset B) \,\&\, A) \supset B), \quad (A \supset (B \supset A)).$$

Thus, by a careful selection among logical truths, it is possible to develop a set of axioms from which other truths of logic can be derived.

Of course, there does seem to be a residual problem. If we are attempting to formalize logic itself, what are we to use in making our derivations? In other words, do we not have to specify rules of inference to be employed in making deductions? The answer is "yes." As our purpose, however, is to systematize, organize, and reduce the subject-matter to basics, we shall try to get the smallest set of inference rules requisite. In fact, it turns out that an axiom system for propositional logic can be described that utilizes just *one* rule of inference. Moreover, it can be shown that the system is sufficient to derive every logical truth of propositional logic. By virtue of having an exactly specified language in which the theory is expressed and a minimal set of basic terms, axioms, and rules of derivation, such a system constitutes a formal, precise theory developed from a basic part of the theory.

It must not be supposed, however, that there is only one set of terms and sentences that is "basic" and, hence, sufficient for logic. Logicians have discovered many such systems. "Basicness" is relative to the system; what is basic and underived in one system may be defined or deduced in another. Axiomatization of logic is important because it permits the exact study of logic and greatly facilitates our ability to gain knowledge about logical systems themselves. Formal presentation of logic, then, is a greatly beneficial tool in advancing our knowledge of logic.[9]

It further turns out that we can greatly expand the power of axiomatization of logic by keeping separate the process of specifying the signs or alphabet of the language of the system, along with its grammar,[10] from the process of specifying the *meaning* or *references* of the symbols used. By developing a theory in this abstract way, without reference to an interpretation or meaning of the signs employed, we greatly expand its utility. Just how this is true will be explained presently. What we need to understand now is what an *uninterpreted* system is and how it is developed. Let us do so with respect to a language we wish eventually to interpret for propositional logic.

We must begin by specifying the "alphabet"—the signs that may occur in the language. They are

$$- \quad \lor \quad (\quad) \quad P_1 \quad P_2 \quad \ldots$$

(The dots at the end indicate that the subscripted letter series continues infinitely; the dots are not part of the alphabet.) Next, we indicate what are *well-formed formulas* of the language. We want eventually to be able to interpret the signs as having meanings appropriate for propositional logic. The interpretation we have in mind is called the *intended interpretation.* The idea, then, is to specify the well-formed formulas in such a way that they coincide, when interpreted, with the symbolic sentences of propositional logic. We must do so, however, only by referring to the signs themselves or their physical interrelationships. Such a specification is called *syntactical,* meaning that it refers only to signs and their interrelations. If we were to refer to relations between signs and other objects in the world or their meanings, the specification would be *semantical.*[11] Our objective is to abstract from meaning, to develop an uninterpreted "language." We must, then, give a syntactical characterization of well-formed formula. We can do so as follows:

(1) Any member of the infinite list P_1, P_2, . . . , alone, is a well-formed formula.

(2) Let A and B be any signs or series of signs from the alphabet; if A is a well-formed formula and B is a well-formed formula, then $(A \lor B)$ is a well-formed formula.

(3) If A is a well-formed formula, then $(-A)$ is a well-formed formula.

(4) Nothing is a well-formed formula unless it follows from 1–3 that it is so.

This definition of 'well-formed formula' enables us to take any signs or series of signs and determine whether they are well-formed formulas simply from their appearance. At this stage it is customary to introduce a set of abbreviations, as follows:

(1) Any formula of the form $((-A) \lor B)$ may be abbreviated by $(A \supset B)$.

(2) Any formula of the form $((-A) \lor (-B))$ may be abbreviated by $(A \mathbin{\&} B)$.

(3) Any formula of the form $((A \supset B) \mathbin{\&} (B \supset A))$ may be abbreviated by $(A \equiv B)$.

These abbreviations are also syntactical in nature, since they permit us to replace strings of signs with others. Also, as the longer expressions may be used to replace the shorter ones, the replacement is not always a true "abbreviation." Once the signs are given meanings in propositional logic, we shall see that each abbreviation permits substitution for one another of propositions that are logically equivalent to one another. The abbreviations facilitate doing proofs and derivations within the system. We can also state any axioms and rules using the abbreviations. The strategy at this stage is to pick out well-formed formulas which, when appropriately interpreted in propositional logic, will be logically true sentences. If we then can specify syntactically a rule that permits our writing new formulas from old ones in such a way that the formulas, when interpreted, are valid consequences of the sentences they are based on, then we shall be able to deduce further logical truths from the axioms.

It is very common in specifying axioms for sentential logic to permit infinitely many, each of which has a particular form. In other words, instead of *listing* the axioms, we give a list of the *forms* of axioms. Any formula having one of these forms is an axiom. Such a list is referred to as a list of *axiom-schemata;* each member of the list is an *axiom-schema.* A common set of axiom-schemata, using the abbreviations, is as follows:

Axiom-schema 1. $((A \lor A) \supset A)$
Axiom-schema 2. $(A \supset (A \lor B))$
Axiom-schema 3. $((A \lor B) \supset (B \lor A))$
Axiom-schema 4. $((A \supset B) \supset ((C \lor A) \supset (C \lor B)))$

A formula is an axiom in the abbreviated language, then, if it is a substitution-instance of one of the axiom-schemata. Strictly speaking, of course, it is the *un*abbreviated formulas that are the axioms, but it is convenient to work with abbreviated expressions.

 We can now state the only rule of "inference" that is needed for sentential logic. We cannot, of course, state this rule referring to validity, since validity is a semantical notion referring to relations among truth-values of statements, while we are dealing solely with meaningless marks. Similarly, the notion of a proof, or derivation, must be specified syntactically. A derivation can be regarded as a sequence of well-formed formulas, each of which is either (i) an axiom, or (ii) derived according to the rule from (two) formulas that occur earlier in the sequence. A *theorem* is any well-formed formula that is the last line of a derivation. The rule can be stated as follows: If a formula A appears in a sequence, and $(A \supset B)$ appears in that sequence, then B may be written below them in the sequence. This rule corresponds to *Modus Ponens* in propositional logic and will be referred to as M.P.

A sample derivation will illustrate how we can prove further theorems (actually theorem-*schemata*) by using this system. The following sequence is a proof-schema of the theorem-schema $(A \lor (-A))$ (note that unnecessary parentheses have been omitted):

(1) $(A \lor A) \supset A$ Ax. 1
(2) $((A \lor A) \supset A) \supset ((-A \lor (A \lor A)) \supset (-A \lor A))$ Ax. 4
(3) $((-A \lor (A \lor A)) \supset (-A \lor A)$ from 1, 2 by M.P.
(4) $(A \supset (A \lor A)) \supset (A \supset A)$ from 1, 2 by M.P.
[Note: (4) is an abbreviation of (3)]
(5) $A \supset (A \lor A)$ Ax. 2
(6) $A \supset A$ from 4, 5 by M.P.
(7) $-A \lor A$ from 4, 5 by M.P.
[(7) is an abbreviation of (6)]
(8) $(-A \lor A) \supset (A \lor -A)$ Ax. 3
(9) $(A \lor -A)$ from 8, 7 by M.P.

Though using such a system is obviously *very* cumbersome and difficult, when the alphabet is interpreted for propositional logic, the result is that all the axioms and theorems derived are logical truths of propositional logic. We give such an interpretation by assigning the normal meanings to the logical constants: V, —, ≡, &, and so on, making the series of subscripted letters sentences and giving a grouping function to the parentheses. We should note, however, that the intended interpretation of an axiomatized system need not be the only possible one. Any interpretation that makes the axioms true will yield a theory of true propositions, so long as the principles of inference chosen are truth-preserving in the interpreted system. Thus, by axiomatizing a body of knowledge as an uninterpreted system, we obtain a very general framework that may well reflect the logical structure of a number of otherwise different subject-matters. Indeed, it is possible to reinterpret the propositional calculus as a theory about electronic switching circuits.[12]

We should make one final point in this section about logical systems such as we have discussed. So far, we have described a system in which it is possible to prove logical truths. Now, we saw that it is possible to do this in systems of natural deduction also. Those systems, however, can also be used to derive conclusions from given premises, thus serving as a test for the validity of arguments and as a tool for discovering the consequences of given premises. Axiomatic logic systems can, in fact, be readily adapted for this purpose also. We simply allow *any* well-formed formula to occur in a proof-sequence as an assumption. We can then readily define the notion of a *proof from assumptions* that corresponds with that of a deduction from premises in natural deduction.

Moreover, whenever we are able to deduce a sentence from another, we are, in effect, saying that the inference of the second from the first is valid. In other words, we are saying that the argument-form exemplified is valid. We can, then, catalogue rules arrived at in this way as *derived rules,* which may be employed in further uses of the system. Each of these rules is, of course, syntactically phrased, so we have not violated the strictures of formalization. Moreover, since the original derivation was done *without* the derived rule, we may be assured that its function is primarily that of simplifying further proofs, unless, of course, our interest is precisely that of seeing what sort of body of inference rules we can generate from our system. The system itself, however, is not *strengthened* from a theoretical point of view, since anything that can be proved with the derived rules could be proved without them. We should note that the Deduction Theorem (see Chapter II, footnote 6), which underlies conditional proof in natural deduction, is a metatheorem about axiomatic systems and is made the basis of a derived rule that is useful in proofs from assumptions. Of course, axiom systems are more cumbersome to work with and somewhat "unnatural." They do, however, facilitate the study of the properties of logical systems. We shall turn now to an account of some of the most important properties of logical systems in which logicians have an interest.

The study of the properties of logical systems is part of metalogic. It is fair to say that metalogic attracts most of the attention of professional logicians. Though an extended treatment of metalogic is beyond our purposes, we can mention several kinds of features of logical systems.

First and foremost of the properties of logical systems is consistency. In particular, an axiom system is said to be *consistent* (according to one definition) if, and only if, it is not the case that both a sentence and a denial of it are theorems. If there is a well-formed formula such that both it and its negation can be derived as theorems from the axioms, then the system is *inconsistent*. Obviously, this is not a desirable property.

The axioms of a system are said to be independent of one another if, and only if, none can be derived from the others. If an axiom is derivable from others, there is nothing terribly wrong with that, but from the point of view of reducing a subject-matter to basic parts such an axiom would be excess baggage.

An axiom system for logic is said to be *complete* if, and only if, every logical truth that can be formulated in the system is provable as a theorem. It can be shown, for example, that the axiom system we have given for sentential logic is complete for logical truth in sentential logic; every logical truth of sentential logic *can* be derived as a theorem from its axioms. Moreover, logicians have demonstrated that there are axiom systems for predicate logic also that are complete; i.e., every logical truth of predicate logic is derivable as a theorem from the axioms. Note, however, that logicians have also demonstrated that though there is a decision-procedure for logical truth in propositional logic, there can be no decision-procedure for logical truth in predicate logic. This means that though every logical truth of predicate logic *can* be proved in the system, there is no mechanical way of coming up with the proof; doing so depends on our luck and cleverness.

The extensions of metalogic and the study of formal deductive theories have been very fruitful. It is worth mentioning one of the most important. In an earlier section we indicated that we can augment basic logic (sentential and first-order logic) in certain ways that permit the axiomatization within the augmented logic of arithmetic. In some sense, such a theory constitutes a reduction of arithmetic to a *foundation*. However, it has been shown that any axiom system for arithmetic that is consistent is also incomplete. That is, certain truths of arithmetic cannot be derived from the axioms! (This proof was given by Kurt Gödel in 1931.) This important result is made possible by the study of formal systems.

4. ALTERNATE TECHNIQUES IN PROPOSITIONAL LOGIC

a. Truth-Tables

Deduction is not the only technique employed in logic. In Chapter I, for example, we sketched very briefly how truth-tables can be employed to test arguments for validity in propositional logic. There are, in fact, four primary uses of truth-tables: (a) to define the connectives, (b) to display the truth-conditions of particular sentences, (c) to test arguments for truth-functional validity, and (d) to test for other properties and relations among statements—e.g., the property of being a logical truth or the relation of being logically equivalent. Virtually all logic texts that cover propositional logic present detailed discussion of such uses of truth-tables, so we shall not do so.

b. Truth-Trees

We turn now to a technique that combines the technique of natural deduction with the graphic features of truth-tables. This method is known as *truth-trees*.[13] It begins with the same insight concerning validity as the indirect proof method—viz., that an argument is valid if, and only if, it is not possible for all the premises and a denial of the conclusion to all be true. To begin with, then, the premises are written down in order, followed by a denial of the conclusion. Let us consider an example:

(1) $-(P \supset -Q)$ Premise
(2) $(Q \supset S)$ Premise
(3) $(-S \lor U)$ Premise
(4) $-(P \& S)$ Denial of the conclusion

We want to see whether this is possible—i.e., whether all these can be true. We do this by tracing out the truth-conditions of each of the sentences. Let us begin with (1). '$-(P \supset -Q)$' is true only if '$(P \supset -Q)$' is false. A conditional sentence is false *only* if the antecedent is true and the consequent false. So, if (1) is true, then 'P' is true, and '$-Q$' is false. We record this as follows:

(5) P
(6) $--Q$

Now let us look at (2). If it is true, then either 'Q' is false or 'S' is true. Since there are two possibilities, we record this fact by indicating two "branches" to our "tree," either of which would make the sentence true:

(7)   −*Q*   *S*

Having completed the truth-conditions of (2), we can now go back up the branches of the tree, in which case we discover that on (7) occurs '−*Q*', and on (6) occurs '−−*Q*'. Since *both* of these cannot be true, we have hit a dead-end on that branch; it does not represent a branch of sentences that would make (1)–(4) all true. We indicate this by placing an 'X' under it. Thus, line (7) will now appear as:

(7)   −*Q*   *S*
              X

We now look at line (3). It is of the form (*A* ∨ *B*) and will be true if *either* '−*S*' or '*U*' is true. We must record this, though we have only one branch to work with, since we have cut off a branch. Thus, (7) and (8) would appear: [14]

(7)   −*Q*   *S*
              X

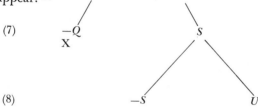

(8)   −*S*   *U*

Again, if we go back up the branches, we discover a contradiction; so again we must cut off the branch on which this happens. We must, then, place an 'X' under '−*S*' on line (8). Assuming we have done this, we turn to line (4). This sentence is '−(*P* & *S*)'. If it is true, then either '*P*' is false or '*S*' is false. We record this as follows:

(8)   −*S*   *U*
              X

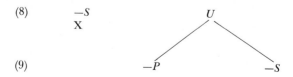

(9)   −*P*   −*S*

If we go back up the left branch, we discover that at (9) occurs

'−*P*', while at (5) is '*P*', so we must cut off *that* branch with an 'X'. If we go up the right branch, we find '−*S*' on (9), and '*S*' on (7), so, again, a branch must be cut off with an 'X'. We have now traced out the truth-conditions of *each* of the original sentences and no branches have been left open. This means there is no branch that represents a set of sentences that, if true, would make all of (1)–(4) true. Thus, we can conclude that the argument is valid. If there *had* been an open branch left—a branch that, at the end, had not been cut off with an 'X'—then we would know the argument was *not* valid, *and* we would know under what conditions the premises could all be true while a denial of the conclusion was also true. We could then easily construct a *counterexample* to the claim that the argument is valid. The entire tree appears as follows:

(1) −(*P* ⊃ −*Q*)   Premise
(2) (*Q* ⊃ *S*)   Premise
(3) (−*S* ∨ *U*)   Premise
(4) −(*P* & *S*)   Denial of the conclusion
(5) *P*

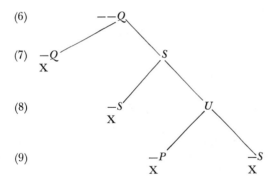

At each step in the construction of the tree we said that if a certain statement was true, then some other statement or statements must be true. In effect, we *inferred* certain sentences from others. By recording the *rules* governing these inferences, we can set up a mechanical method for writing out truth-trees that will always give us an answer to the question of an argument's validity. These rules are neatly summarized as follows:

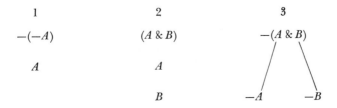

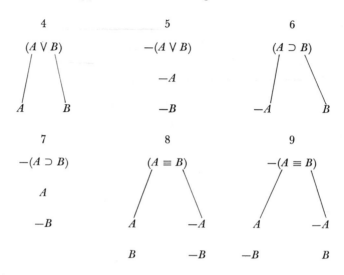

All we need now are rules telling us to apply these rules at each step and how to cut off contradictory branches, and we have then described a method to test arguments for validity [15] that is a mechanical, effective decision-procedure for validity. We should note further that the method can be applied to very complex sentences, taken singly, breaking them down by means of a tree to letters and letters preceded by dashes. If it is possible for the sentence to be true, at least one branch will remain open. Thus, truth-trees can be used to test whether a sentence is *self-consistent.* Suppose, on the other hand, we negate a sentence, construct its tree, and discover that *no* branch is left open. *That* sentence, then, *cannot* be true, in which case the original sentence is a logical truth. Truth-trees, then, provide a decision-procedure for logical truth, also. Let us quickly demonstrate the precedure by showing the sentence '$P \supset (-Q \supset P)$' to be a logical truth:

(1) $-(P \supset (-Q \supset P))$
(2) P ⎫
(3) $-(-Q \supset P)$ ⎬ from (1) by rule 7
(4) $-Q$ ⎫
(5) $-P$ ⎬ from (3) by rule 7
        X

c. Normal Forms

The final set of techniques we shall outline utilize what are called *disjunctive normal form* and *conjunctive normal form.* Every sentence of propositional logic *has* a disjunctive normal form and a conjunctive normal form. What this means is that every sentence of propositional logic is logically equivalent to a sentence that is in disjunctive normal form and to one that is in conjunctive normal form. If a sentence is logically equivalent to another, then they *imply* one another. Thus, if one is a logical truth, so is the other. On the other hand, if one is a contradiction, so is the other. The utility of the normal forms is that by merely looking at them we can tell whether or not they are logically true or false. Thus, if we can devise a method for finding an equivalent normal form for a sentence, we have a way of testing the sentence for logical truth or falsehood. Moreover, since the validity of arguments can be defined in terms of the logical truth of a corresponding conditional, the same test will serve as a test of validity. Let us now explain the normal forms and how this all works.

First, it can be easily shown that any statement expressed in the symbolism of propositional logic is logically equivalent to a sentence containing only '−', 'V', and '&'. Moreover, each sentence is equivalent to one meeting the following conditions: (a) it has no connectives other than those in the list just given; (b) 'V' occurs only between single letters or negations of single letters (if at all); (c) '−' applies only to single letters (if it occurs). A sentence that meets these conditions is in *conjunctive normal form*. If one looks carefully over these conditions, he will discover that any sentence in conjunctive normal form is either (i) a single letter or a negation of a single letter, or (ii) a series of conjunctions, each conjunct of which is either a single letter, a negation of a single letter, or a disjunction of single letters or their negations, or (iii) a series of such disjunctions. Each of the following is in conjunctive normal form:

$((P \lor Q) \mathbin{\&} (R \lor S))$
$(P \lor W)$
$(P \mathbin{\&} Q)$
$(((P \lor Q) \lor R) \mathbin{\&} ((P \lor R) \lor Q))$
$((P \lor Q) \mathbin{\&} R)$

A sentence is in *disjunctive normal form* if, and only if, it meets the following conditions: (a) it has no connectives other than '−', 'V', and '&'; (b) '−' applies only to single letters; (c) the '&' sign occurs only between single letters or their negations. Given these conditions, each of the following is in disjunctive normal form:

$(P \lor Q)$
$(((P \mathbin{\&} Q) \mathbin{\&} R) \lor -S)$
$((P \mathbin{\&} Q) \lor (R \mathbin{\&} S))$
$(P \mathbin{\&} Q)$
$((P \lor Q) \lor S)$

Normally a sentence in *conjunctive* normal form will appear as a conjunction, each conjunct of which is a disjunction of single letters or negations of single letters. Normally a sentence in *disjunctive* normal form will appear as a disjunction, each disjunct of which is a conjunction of single letters or negations of single letters. Thus, the framework of a sentence in conjunctive normal form will be like this: (__ V __) & (__ V __). The framework of a disjunctive normal form will be like this: (__ & __) V (__ & __). A bit of reflection will show that the following is true: a sentence in conjunctive normal form is *logically true* if, and only if, in *each* disjunction there occurs both a single letter and its negation. (Since a sentence in conjunctive normal form is a series of conjuncts, it can be logically true only if *each* conjunct is logically true.) Similarly, the following will be the case: a sentence in disjunctive normal form is *logically false* if, and only if, each disjunct contains a single letter and its negation.

The only problem remaining with this technique is to describe how to *find* a disjunctive or conjunctive normal form for a given sentence. Without giving detailed instructions, we can indicate that such a procedure is readily developed by permitting the substitution for one another of sentences having the forms indicated in each of the following logically equivalent pairs:

(1) $(A \lor B)$ and $(B \lor A)$
(2) $(A \& B)$ and $(B \& A)$
(3) $((A \lor B) \lor C)$ and $(A \lor (B \lor C))$
(4) $((A \& B) \& C)$ and $(A \& (B \& C))$
(5) $(A \& (B \lor C))$ and $((A \& B) \lor (A \& C))$
(6) $(A \lor (B \& C))$ and $((A \lor B) \& (A \lor C))$
(7) A and $--A$
(8) $-(A \& B)$ and $(-A \lor -B)$
(9) $-(A \lor B)$ and $(-A \& -B)$
(10) $(A \supset B)$ and $(-A \lor B)$
(11) $(A \equiv B)$ and $((-A \lor B) \& (-B \lor A))$

By successive applications of these rules for making substitutions, we can take any sentence and "reduce" it to one of the normal forms. This technique has the obvious disadvantage that it is extremely cumbersome to apply and use. It is important, however, for two reasons. First, it is possible to give a step-by-step procedure for making the reduction that could be programmed onto a machine and that would give correct answers to questions of logical truth and validity in propositional logic. Second, reduction to normal form is an extremely useful tool in metalogical proofs about the properties of logic systems.[16]

5. SOME NOTES ON PREDICATE LOGIC

a. Further Symbolism and Interpretations

Thus far in this chapter we have utilized the symbolism and techniques of propositional logic only. While it is beyond the scope of this book to develop advanced areas of logic, it is possible to outline the basic symbolism of predicate logic and to describe techniques for its simplest branches.

The most important difference between propositional and predicate logic is that predicate logic is concerned with the internal structure of individual statements. The simplest sort of internal structure to understand is that of a sentence that mentions a particular thing and says it has a certain characteristic—e.g., 'The Empire State Building has a pointed top' or 'Leontyne Price is an opera star'. Such a sentence is said to be a *singular* sentence or statement. In it is an expression referring to a particular thing and a characterizing term or phrase, which the logician calls a *predicate*. The logician's use of this term includes verbs and noun phrases, as well as adjectives. Any term or phrase that is used to ascribe a property or relation to some thing or things is a predicate.[17] To symbolize singular statements, the logician requires symbols for individual terms and symbols for the predicates. It is common to use lower-case letters from the beginning of the alphabet, $a, b, \ldots , i$ (applying numerical subscripts if more are needed), to refer to individual things and upper-case letters to refer to properties. Thus, to symbolize 'Leontyne Price is an opera star' we might use:

Oa

Here, 'a' refers to Leontyne Price, 'O' to the property of being an opera star. The order of reference is the reverse of the English order. (Though there is little justification for this, it is the custom.) Since each letter has a definite referent, each is called a *constant*; 'a' is an *individual* constant, 'O' a *predicate* constant.

Suppose we delete the reference to Leontyne Price, but we want the predicate symbol to reflect the fact that it is one-place. We could put a place-holder in for 'a'—i.e., an expression having no definite reference and to be replaced by an individual constant. We can use the lower-case letters 'w' through 'z' (applying numerical subscripts if more are needed) as such place-holders. As these do not refer to particular things, and various terms can be used to replace them, they are called *individual variables* (or just *variables*). So we can indicate the logical role of '*O*' as one-place by writing:

   Ox

Now, the expression we have written is not a sentence or sentence-abbreviation. We could make it a sentence-abbreviation (we shall say *sentence* from now on) by replacing '*x*' with '*a*'. '*Ox*' has the same function as '___ is an opera star'; this becomes a sentence if the blank is replaced with an expression referring to someone. In other words, '*Ox*' is a *sentence-form*,[18] and any sentence that is the result of replacing '*x*' in the form with an individual constant is a *substitution-instance* of '*Ox*'.

   There is another way the logician makes a sentence out of sentence-forms. This is to preface the sentence-form with a *quantifier*. Suppose we wrote:

   There is an *x*, such that *x* is an opera star.

This is not quite English, but one might well understand it to assert:

   There is something such that it is an opera star.

or

   Something (or someone) is an opera star.

Similarly, we would probably understand someone who wrote:

   For any *x*, *x* is an opera star.

to mean the same as

   Everything (or everyone) is an opera star.

Two further symbolic conventions are adopted, then. '(∃*x*)' is used to mean (roughly) "there is an *x* such that," and '(*x*)' is used to mean "for any *x*." Thus, we can take the sentence-form '*Ox*' and make a sentence of it in two new ways:

   (∃*x*)*Ox*
   (*x*)*Ox*

The first sentence says that there is at least one opera star; the second says that everything is an opera star. The symbol '(*x*)' is called the *universal* quantifier. '(∃*x*)' is called the *existential* quantifier.

Aside from the usual connectives from propositional logic, all that is needed now is a way of symbolizing relational predicates—e.g., 'is a brother of', 'is between', and so on. Suppose we let '*B*' stand for the relation of being a brother of. We can write a sentence-form for it that brings out its relational character as follows:

Bxy

This can become a sentence in several ways. First, we can replace '*x*' and '*y*' with individual constants. Were this done, the sentence would say that two particular people are brothers. Suppose we let '*a*' stand for James Jones. Then the following would be a sentence also:

$(\exists x)\,Bax$

This sentence says that James Jones is someone's brother. The following would also be a sentence:

$(\exists x)(\exists y)Bxy$

This says that there is someone who is a brother to someone.

We can illustrate how the new symbolism is employed by showing how the traditional **A, E, I,** and **O** statements are symbolized. This is done below: [19]

A	**E**	**I**	**O**
All *F* are *G*.	No *F* are *G*.	Some *F* are *G*.	Some *F* are not *G*.
$(x)(Fx \supset Gx)$	$(x)(Fx \supset -Gx)$	$(\exists x)(Fx \,\&\, Gx)$	$(\exists x)(Fx \,\&\, -Gx)$

Something should also be said concerning the interpretation of the symbolism. Usually, if we are working with a particular argument or group of arguments, it is convenient to assume that we are not speaking about everything whatever. We can, then, specify a *universe of discourse*— a class of objects—which are taken as candidates to be named by individual constants. If the universe of discourse is the class of persons, then a sentence such as '$(x)(Fx \supset Gx)$' is taken to mean that all *persons* who have a certain property have a further property. At the most informal level we usually just assume a universe of discourse and assign lower-case letters to individuals named in the argument and let upper-case letters to stand in for the English predicates that occur. The interpretation of the symbolism can, however, be made more comprehensive and explicit, and there is a standard manner of specifying an interpretation for the symbolism.

We give a standard interpretation by first specifying a nonempty class of objects—called the *domain*—which is the universe of discourse. Individual constants are assigned to objects in the domain, which the constants then name. One-place predicates are interpreted as designating subclasses of objects in the domain. (If the domain is the positive integers, we could let '*P*' stand for the class having as members the infinite series: 2, 4, 6, 8, ... '*P*' would then stand in for the predicate 'even number'.) Two-place predicates are assigned classes of ordered pairs of objects from the domain. Three-place predicates are assigned classes of ordered triples, and so on. Sentence letters ('*P*', '*Q*', and so on, written without accompanying variables or constants) are assigned truth or falsity.

An interpretation under which a given sentence, or group of sentences, is true is said to be a *model* of the sentence or sentences. The study of interpretations and their properties, known as *model theory*, has become a very important part of modern logic. Many of the important concepts of logic—e.g., logical consequence—are semantic concepts and they can be given definitions that refer to models or interpretations.[20] Moreover, there have been important discoveries in the theory of interpretations that have great significance for developing proof and disproof techniques. One important discovery is known as the *Löwenheim-Skolem* theorem. This says, essentially, that any first-order logical system that has a model at all also has a model with the positive integers as the domain or universe of discourse. While this theorem has enormous theoretical importance, part of its practical significance is that we can often concentrate attention on simple arithmetical models that are easy to deal with.

We shall now briefly describe the sorts of techniques employed in predicate logic. A detailed presentation of these techniques is beyond the purposes of this book.

b. Techniques in Predicate Logic

For the most part, the techniques available in predicate logic are extensions of those available in propositional logic. The chief ones we shall describe are: Venn diagrams, normal forms, inference rules, and semantic tableaux (or truth-trees).

Venn diagrams are presented in most logic texts because they are easily learned, graphically illustrate logical relationships, and are adequate for all syllogistic arguments and further kinds, as well. The diagrams are made up of overlapping circles, drawn in a way to represent or display certain class relationships. Several kinds of diagrams work in this way, but the most widely used are those of the English logician, John Venn, who devised them in the late nineteenth century.[21]

A more complicated, but more widely applicable sort of test consists in constructing the corresponding conditional for an argument and then testing it for logical truth by a method similar to that of reduction to a normal form. Such a technique can be developed as a decision-procedure for all of monadic predicate logic,[22] and such methods are available for certain kinds of sentences in polyadic predicate logic.

The most widely used technique in general predicate logic involves adding inference rules to the system of deduction. The new rules govern sentences containing the quantifiers. Virtually all logic texts present a system of deduction for predicate logic, so we shall not attempt to duplicate them. Moreover, different ways of stating restrictions for certain of the rules can be confusing to the student.

Finally, we should mention that we can add to the rules for truth-trees and extend that method to predicate logic. The general method is known as the method of *semantic tableaux*.[23] This technique can also be used as a decision-procedure for monadic predicate logic. While it can be applied to polyadic predicate logic, it cannot be used as more than a partial test of validity.

6. ALTERNATE SYMBOLS AND NOTATIONS

Over the years the symbols used by logicians have proliferated. The table below shows ways of writing formulas that are used as alternatives to one another. In the lefthand column are the symbolizations used in this book. To the right are the alternatives.

$-P$	$\sim P$	$\neg P$	$\overline{P}$
$(P \& Q)$	$(P \cdot Q)$	PQ	$P \vee Q$
$(P \vee Q)$	$(P + Q)$		
$(P \supset Q)$	$(P \longrightarrow Q)$		
$(P \equiv Q)$	$(P \longleftrightarrow Q)$		
$(x)Fx$	$\vee xFx$	$\prod xFx$	$\vee xFx$
$(\exists x)Fx$	$\vee xFx$	$\sum xFx$	

Moreover, there are grouping notations alternative to the use of parentheses. One notation, with several variants, employs *more* grouping symbols, e.g., $\{[\quad]\}$. Thus, what we would write as $((P \supset Q) \vee (R \supset (S \& T)))$ might be written as $\{(P \supset Q) \vee [R \supset (S \& T)]\}$. The additional symbols may provide clearer visual clues as to the proper grouping.

Other notations dispense with parentheses entirely and are known as *parentheses-free* notations. The most common of these combine the use of dots in place of parentheses with a convention that assigns an order of "binding strength" to the connectives. To illustrate such a convention, '—' is taken as applying to the shortest sentence it can be read as attaching to, and '&' is taken as having less binding force than any other two-place connective; i.e., when it occurs without parentheses, it joins only the letters (negated or otherwise) beside it. Thus, '$-P$ & Q' would abbreviate '$(-P$ & $Q)$', and 'P & Q ∨ R' would abbreviate '$((P$ & $Q)$ ∨ $R)$'. Indeed, if the connectives are all arranged in an order of binding strength, the use of parentheses can be cut down considerably. Usually, however, this device is combined with a dot notation; i.e., dots are used in place of parentheses. The simplest technique consists in assigning an order of strength to the following kinds of dot configurations:

$$. \quad : \quad \therefore \quad ::$$

To mark the main break in a sentence the largest group of dots is used, and so on. Thus, the sentence '$((P ⊃ Q) ∨ (P ⊃ (R$ & $S)))$' would be written:

$$P ⊃ Q : ∨ : P ⊃ \quad R \& S$$

A further device, invented by the Polish logician Łukasiewicz (in 1929), dispenses entirely with parentheses and abbreviations for them. This device, known as *Polish notation,* consists in placing a letter representing a connective *before* the sentence it joins. The following table shows how this is done. As the notation is clearer if lower-case letters are used for sentence-abbreviations, this has been done:

$-p$	Np
$(p ∨ q)$	Apq
$(p$ & $q)$	Kpq
$(p ⊃ q)$	Cpq
$(p ≡ q)$	Epq

Using this notation, we write the sentence '$((p ∨ q) ⊃ (r ⊃ (s$ & $t)))$' as '$CApqCrKst$'. One merely has to look at the first upper-case letter to tell the main connective. In this case we know the whole sentence is a conditional. Since 'A' occurs immediately after 'C', we know the antecedent is a disjunction (or "alternation"), and since that disjunction is made up of 'p' and 'q', the consequent of the main conditional must be the next large, compound sentence. It is a conditional with 'r' as antecedent and 'Kst' as consequent. Polish notation is not widely used in logic texts and only somewhat more widely used in technical work. Logicians who first learned logic with the more traditional symbolism often complain that the Polish notation is difficult for them to read. The utility of the notation seems ultimately to rest on what one feels comfortable with.

NOTES

1. This is one commonly employed set of symbols. Books differ somewhat in this respect. A table of alternative symbols is found at the end of this chapter.
2. There are other ways to accomplish this purpose. Sometimes small letters are used to abbreviate sentences and capitals are used for displaying sentence-forms (or vice versa). Sometimes the distinction is marked by using boldface type and lighter type.
3. The explanation here follows somewhat the presentation found in Robert Neidorf, *Deductive Forms: An Elementary Logic* (New York: Harper & Row, 1967).
4. We can explain this in more explicit terms. A statement, A, is *logically equivalent* to a statement, B, if, and only if, it is necessarily the case that A and B have the same truth-value. It follows, then, that if $(A \equiv B)$ is logically true, then A and B are logically equivalent. Moreover, A and B are logically equivalent if, and only if, A implies B and B implies A.
5. 'Contains' is meant in a broad way—a sentence contains itself as well as every proper part of itself.
6. This procedure presupposes the truth of the following statement: A set of statements $A_1, A_2, \ldots, A_n$ logically implies a statement of the form $(B \supset C)$ if, and only if, $A_1, A_2, \ldots, A_n$ together with B, logically imply C. This statement is sometimes called *the deduction theorem*. The role of the deduction theorem in axiom systems is discussed in the section that follows.
7. Mathematics students are probably familiar with the use of indirect proof to show that something (e.g., a number of a certain kind) does or does not exist. Such proofs, known as *existence proofs*, save considerable time.
8. Rudolf Carnap has given outlines for the axiomatization of various theories in arithmetic, geometry, physics, biology, and legal theory. See his book, *Introduction to Symbolic Logic and its Applications* (New York: Dover Publications, Inc., 1958).
9. We should quickly add, however, that axiomatic systems are not nearly so useful in doing everyday logic problems, unless they are made more like natural deduction systems by the addition of "derived" rules of inference.
10. By the 'grammar' of a language, in the logician's sense, is meant the rules specifying acceptable combinations of the alphabet. In this sense of the word, the "grammar" of English sanctions the sentence 'The cat is in the house' but does not sanction 'The house cat in is'. Similarly, it sanctions 'cat' but does not sanction 'cta'.
11. The terminology used here is due to Charles W. Morris, who distinguished the following relationships signs can have: (1) *syntactical*—relations among

signs themselves, (2) *semantical*—relations between signs and objects, (3) *pragmatical*—relations between signs and their users. See his monograph, *Foundations of the Theory of Signs* (Chicago: University of Chicago Press, 1938).

12. How this is done is described in Samuel D. Guttenplan and Martin Tamny, *Logic: A Comprehensive Introduction* (New York: Basic Books, 1971), pp. 143–147.

13. Truth-trees derive from work on a method called "semantic tableaux" developed by the Dutch logician E. W. Beth. The method presented here derives largely from a book that systematically employs truth-trees throughout: R. C. Jeffrey, *Formal Logic: Its Scope and Limits* (New York: McGraw-Hill Book Company, 1967).

14. Note that if the branch ending in '−Q' at line (7) had not been cut off, we would have to repeat our two options under it.

15. A concise statement of the rules is to be found in Guttenplan and Tamny, *Logic,* p. 129.

16. Normal forms are especially important in completeness proofs in propositional logic. A lucid completeness proof using normal forms is outlined in Robert Neidorf, *Deductive Forms,* chap. IV.

17. An excellent discussion of the differences between the logician's and the grammarian's use of the term 'predicate' is to be found in Jack Kaminsky and Alice Kaminsky, *Logic: A Philosophical Introduction* (Reading, Mass.: Addison-Wesley Publishing Company, 1974), p. 150.

18. What we are calling sentence-forms in predicate logic are also called *open sentences.* A somewhat older designation is *propositional functions.*

19. Note that, using these symbolizations, the **A** and **E** statements will both be true if there is nothing that is an *F.* This differs from the traditional treatment and is discussed in Chapter IV. The traditional view is said to assume the *existential import* of the **A** and **E** statements.

20. A brief example: a sentence *A* implies a sentence *B* if, and only if, any interpretation that is a model of *A* is also a model of *B.*

21. An accessible and clearly presented outline of Venn diagrams is to be found in Wesley C. Salmon, *Logic,* 2d ed., Foundations of Philosophy Series (Englewood Cliffs, N.J.: Prentice-Hall, Inc., 1973), pp. 59–70.

22. Such a procedure is described in W. V. Quine, *Methods of Logic,* 3d ed. (New York: Holt, Rinehart and Winston, Inc., 1972), pp. 129–134.

23. The method is fully described in Jeffrey, *Formal Logic,* and in Guttenplan and Tamny, *Logic,* pp. 210–223.

III

Some Further Topics
in the Philosophy of Logic

At this stage of the student's exposure to modern deductive logic it should be evident that a number of highly debatable matters arise in that study. Some of these (for example, the question of the manner in which truths of logic are known) have already been discussed in this book. The list of such problems and difficulties is, however, quite long. Some of these issues may have occurred to the student already or been mentioned in the student's textbook of logic. In this chapter we shall take up several further problems in order to acquaint the student more fully with the nature of such difficulties and some of the standard ways of treating them. Some of these problems can be understood and discussed without presupposing a great deal of logical facility or background. Of course, these discussions are somewhat incomplete, so the interested student should look at the materials listed in our bibliography and notes for additional study.

1. THE NATURE OF LOGICAL IMPLICATION

a. The Material Conditional

Implication is one of the most important relations the logician studies. In a valid argument the premises are said to logically imply the conclusion, and if a group of sentences logically implies a sentence, then an argument is valid that has the sentences in the group as premises and the implied sentence as conclusion. So the concepts of deductive validity and logical implication are intimately connected and are central to logical theory. Over the years, however, there has been some controversy concerning the nature of logical implication. The manner in which the controversy arises can be illustrated by discussing a confusion sometimes made between the meaning of '⊃' and logical implication. Indeed, most beginning textbooks give the reader some warning about this confusion—it is quite infamous—so what we shall say may already be somewhat familiar.

The sign '⊃' (or some other variant) is employed in contemporary logic as a translation of the English expression 'If __, then __'. That is, a statement of the form 'If *A,* then *B*', is regularly symbolized as '(*A* ⊃ *B*)'. There are problems with this. Recall that '⊃' is defined contextually; i.e., we define it by specifying truth-conditions for all sentences containing it. In particular, we define it in such a way that any sentence of the form (*A* ⊃ *B*) is taken to be false *only* if *A* is true and *B* is false. The first difficulty this creates (which we shall discuss later) is that it hardly seems an accurate translation of ordinary English statements of the form 'If *A,* then *B*'. Consider the statement 'If I visit Disneyland tomorrow, I shall get a million dollars'. Would one be willing to say this is true *because* one knows one will not visit Disneyland and will not get a million dollars? Yet, if we symbolize that statement as '(*A* ⊃ *B*)', we *must* regard it as true, given the way in which '⊃' has been defined. Whether there can be any justification for such a symbolization is a question to which we shall return later. A further problem is connected with the use of '⊃' to symbolize 'If __, then __' statements.

In ordinary discourse (according to some logicians) there is a close connection between some uses of 'If __, then __' and logical implication. Sometimes (in their view) we use the expression 'If __, then __' to indicate there is a logical connection between the sentences that go in the blanks. 'If John or Mary was home, and Mary was not, then John was at home' may carry the sense that there is a necessary connection between the first (compound) sentence and the second—i.e., that the first logically implies the second. Of course, the 'If __, then __' locution does not always carry such a sense; in fact, it rarely does. 'If I visit Disneyland tomorrow, I shall get a million dollars' would not be taken to have such a sense. Anyone seriously asserting this would be taken as implying not that there is a *necessary* connection between visiting Disneyland and obtaining a large sum of money, but that because of certain contingent circumstances, the visit will have such a result—e.g., if such a visit would result in winning a prize. Such a conditional sentence in ordinary discourse is said to be a *causal conditional*—i.e., true because of contingent happenings and causal laws that connect them. In certain fields of intellectual interest, such as mathematics, conditional assertions are never causal. This fact, together with the use of 'If __, then __' to assert a relation of implication, has sometimes seduced logicians into reading '⊃' as 'implies'.

Now, a statement of the form $(A \supset B)$ is said to be a *material conditional*. A material conditional is, in a sense, weaker than a causal conditional, since it asserts less. A material conditional is true so long as it is not the case that the antecedent is true and the consequent false. A causal conditional requires *more* than this for it to be true; there must, in addition, be a causal *connection* between the antecedent and the consequent. An 'If ___, then ___' statement carrying the sense of a logical relationship is even stronger than this. It tells us that if the antecedent clause is true, then the consequent *could not* be false. It asserts a *necessary connection*. Since the material conditional makes no such claim—it is true so long as it happens not to be the case that the antecedent is true and the consequent false—it is a mistake to read '$\supset$' as 'implies'.

That this is an error has been thought to be illustrated in another way. 'Implies' and equivalent expressions, such as 'entails', 'logically necessitates', and so on, are often taken as the converse of the relation 'is deducible from'. (As we shall see in the following section, this may be a mistake.) If A entails B, then B is deducible from A. But the mere fact that $(A \supset B)$ is true does not entitle us to deduce B from A. If 'A' is replaced with 'I shall visit Disneyland tomorrow' and 'B' with 'I shall get a million dollars', $(A \supset B)$ will be true because I shall not visit Disneyland tomorrow, yet no one could think to conclude that therefore the consequent is *deducible* from the antecedent.[1] To read '$\supset$' as 'implies', then, yields results that seem not to accord with our understanding of 'implies'. These results are summarized in what are sometimes called the "Paradoxes of Material Implication":

(1)   A false statement implies every statement.

(2)   A true statement is implied by every statement.

These are easily shown. If A is a false statement, then $(A \supset B)$ is true, regardless of what sentence we put in for B, since the material conditional is false *only* if the antecedent is true and the consequent false. Similarly, if B is true, then $(A \supset B)$ is true, no matter what sentence is put in for A, since even if A is true, we will not have a true antecedent and false consequent. Of course, there is nothing "paradoxical" about (1) and (2); they are simply falsehoods if 'implies' is taken to mean 'logically implies'. Some logicians say in this case that A *materially implies* B, and some, in addition, are willing to read '$\supset$' as 'materially implies'.[2] These moves are made in order to distinguish the case where $(A \supset B)$ is true from the case where A logically implies B.

We can add a further point concerning the differences between '$\supset$' and 'implies'. Many logicians, such as W. V Quine, think that this point marks an important difference. When we say that one statement implies another, we are saying something about those *statements.* To talk about statements we must use expressions that refer to those statements in some way. Thus, 'implies' is written between two expressions that name or describe sentences or statements. 'Implies', then, always connects nouns or noun-phrases. '⊃', however, has an entirely different function. Its standard use is to connect sentences, not noun-phrases. The new sentence that results is "about" whatever the constituent sentences are about. '⊃' is a part of a (symbolic) vocabulary that can be used to talk about the world in general, while 'implies' is part of our metalogical vocabulary and is always used to assert that a logical relationship holds among or between statements. 'Implies' is said to be "metalinguistic"—part of a language for talking about language—while '⊃' is part of the language used in talking about things in general.

Let us turn now to attempts to define implication in ways that avoid the difficulties of material implication.

b. Strict Implication

The definition of logical implication given earlier in this book [3] is the one most often used by philosophers and logicians. A statement *A* logically implies a statement *B* if, and only if, it is not possible for *A* to be true while *B* is false. And a group of statements implies a statement *B* if, and only if, it is not possible for all the statements in the group to be true while *B* is false. Thus, if *A* implies *B*, then, if *A* is true, then (necessarily) *B* is true, also.

The utility of this definition is displayed in contrasting it with the use of the '⊃' in forming material conditionals. Consider the following statements: 'John F. Kennedy was President of the United States' and 'Joe Namath played for the New York Jets in 1973'. These are, to be sure, true statements. Let's abbreviate the first by '*P*' and the second by '*Q*'. A conditional of the two can be written as '(*P* ⊃ *Q*)'. Since the antecedent is true and the consequent is true, the conditional is true. But, of course, '*P*' does not imply '*Q*'. This accords with our definition. Since '*P*' *could* have been false as well as true (if, for example, Kennedy had lost the election), and '*Q*' could have been false, e.g., if the Jets had failed to offer their quarterback a sufficiently attractive contract for 1973, *possible* assignments of truth-values to '*P*' and '*Q*' must cover all these possibilities. The truth-table for '(*P* ⊃ *Q*)' would include a row that makes '*P*' true and '*Q*' false. The *actual* circumstance is that both are true. But it is possible for '*P*' to be true and '*Q*' false. Thus, '*P*' does not logically imply '*Q*', even though '(*P* ⊃ *Q*)' is true. This shows that a statement of the form (*A* ⊃ *B*) can be true even though *A* does not imply *B*. Still, there is a connection between conditional sentences and logical implication. We spoke of this in Chapter 1 but did not demonstrate the point.

Let us suppose we have a conditional sentence that is *logically* true. In that case it is not possible for the antecedent to be true while the consequent is false. But, if it is not possible for the antecedent to be true and the consequent false, then (according to our definition of implication) the antecedent *implies* the consequent. We can show the relationship works the other way, too; if a statement implies another, then the conditional is logically true. Suppose A implies B. Then it is not possible for A to be true and B false. In that case, it is not possible for the antecedent in $(A \supset B)$ to be true while the consequent is false. But then that conditional is logically true. (Where a *group* of statements implies a given statement, we take as antecedent a conjunction of all the statements in the group.) We can say, then, that A logically implies B if, and only if, $(A \supset B)$ is logically true. This result seems to accord well with our intuitions concerning implication, since it maintains a logical connection if, and only if, there is some necessary connection among the truth-values of the statements being related. Moreover, to say that $(A \supset B)$ is logically true is to assert something about a statement and is thus a metalogical statement.

In these respects the definition has an advantage over the use of '$\supset$' read as 'implies'. There are grounds, however, on which some logicians have based the claim that even this definition does not capture the ordinary sense of 'implies'. We can elucidate these grounds by considering the following "laws" of implication established using our definition:

(1)   Every statement implies itself.

(2)   If a statement A implies a statement B, and B implies a statement C, then A implies C.

(3)   A logically false statement implies every statement.

(4)   A logically true statement is implied by every statement.

Each of these is easily argued for using the definition of logical implication. Yet, each has seemed to some philosophers to be objectionable —i.e., not to accord with their sense of logical implication. First of all, if implication is to be the basis of inference, it has been maintained that (1) must be rejected, since there can be no real *inference* of a statement from itself.[4] And, of course, if (1) is rejected, then so must (2) be rejected. A statement of the form $(A \lor B)$ surely implies one of the form $(-A \supset B)$. And, the latter implies one of the form $(A \lor B)$. But, if (1) is rejected, we cannot conclude that the first statement implies the third, since they are identical.

It must be said that very few logicians have found such arguments appealing. The claims rest on taking implication, first, to express a relation involving inference, and second, to be based on an analysis of a certain psychological process. But the laws of the basic concepts of logic are regarded as independent of psychology.

In fact, the last two laws have generated considerable criticism, for they seem to produce faulty results in much the same way that reading '⊃' as 'implies' does. Consider the following statements:

(5)   It is raining, or it is not raining.

(6)   The A's won the World Series in 1974, and the A's did not win win the World Series in 1974.

(7)   New York City has the largest population of any city in the United States.

Given the laws of implication, each of the following is true:

(8)   (6) implies (7).

(9)   (7) implies (5).

(10)   (6) implies (5).

What has seemed to many wrong about such a notion of implication is that it appears to us to assert a logical implication between statements that *have no connection* with one another. (7) is (in some sense) "about" the city of New York, while (5) has to do with the weather. How *could* the one imply the other? Similarly, (6) is "about" a baseball team and its performance in the World Series, while (7) is "about" the size of the population of New York in relation to other American cities. The first objection, then, is that given the ordinary sense of 'implies', a statement can imply another only if there is a "connection" between them; only if the first statement is "relevant" to the implied statement. A commonly offered account of that connection is given in terms of meaning. A statement, it is said, implies another only if the *meaning* of the first includes the meaning of the second.[5]

A second objection is that if we accept the "laws" of implication given above, we cannot distinguish good from bad arguments that establish logical truths. Sometimes we need to be *shown* that a logical truth *is* such, and not any valid argument will do. On the other hand, if an argument is valid in which the premises imply the conclusion, and 'imply' is defined as above, then *any* argument is valid that has that logical truth as its conclusion.

The most influential response to such criticisms in modern times has been given by the American logician and philosopher, C. I. Lewis, though it must be said that the entire controversy goes back to ancient times, and

Lewis' arguments (along with the others) are anticipated in earlier literature.[6] Lewis defined a notion, which he called *strict implication,* which is essentially like ours. Lewis symbolized 'strictly implies' with the symbol '-3' and defined it as follows:

'A -3 B' means 'It is not possible that A and $-B$'.

Lewis called attention to the supposedly "paradoxical" results of utilizing this definition, but he thought they are simply easily overlooked truths about the implication relation and not results that require rejecting the definition. How would one go about showing this? To begin with, Lewis pointed out that he intended 'implies' to signify the converse of the relation signified by 'is-deductible-from by some valid mode(s) of inference'. If he could show, then, that given any logically false statement, any conclusion one chooses can be deduced from it, using only valid modes of inference, his point would have been made. Similarly, he could establish the other controversial law if he could show that for any statement at all, there is a deduction from it, using only valid modes of inference, for any logically true statement.

We shall reconstruct Lewis' argument to show that a logically false statement implies any statement at all. Suppose A and B are any statements at all. We shall proceed to derive B from $(A \& -A)$. Let us take $(A \& -A)$ as the premise of an argument:

(1) $(A \& -A)$

From (1) we can deduce:

(2) A

From (1) we can also deduce:

(3) $-A$

From (2) we can deduce:

(4) $(A \lor B)$

From (4) and (3) we can deduce:

(5) B

Lewis presented a similar argument to show that from any statement, a logically true statement can be deduced. Of what significance are these "proofs?" Lewis held that insofar as the point at issue involves a basic concept of logic, the only possible argument consists in tracing out and making explicit the implications of the position we take and testing these against our logical intuitions. *Any* argument will presuppose logical principles. Lewis' proofs are attempts, then, to show that the controversial deductions *can* be made using principles of logic we presuppose in reasoning as valid. In the argument above, the move from (1) to (2) and from (1) to (3) is, in each case, sanctioned by the well-known principle of Simplification which entitles us to deduce either conjunct from a conjunction. The deduction of (4) from (2) is warranted by the principle of Addition. (This principle may be questionable if 'V' is taken as having the exact meaning of the English 'or', but the truth-functional (A V B) raises no such problem.) Finally, the deduction of (5) appeals to the principle of Disjunctive Syllogism. Lewis rhetorically asks his reader whether any of these is a principle he or she would be willing to be deprived of in making inferences, say, in geometry; and, of course, he supposes his readers' logical intuitions on the matter will support his own. Many logicians, however, seem to have contrary intuitions.

Even if we reject Lewis considerable reliance on the appeal to intuition, his proofs make an important point. They demonstrate that if we reject the controversial laws of strict implication, we must also reject, or at least severely restrict, certain patterns of inference that have been widely recognized and utilized in logic over the centuries. If we are to accept an alternative account of implication that avoids the unwanted implications, we shall want to know what corresponding logical system is consistent with it, and how well it can function in guiding inferences. Does it result in rejecting obviously valid arguments? Does it have its own paradoxical results? Is it too cumbersome to use?

Lewis believed that *other* relationships among statements *could* be made the basis of inference and taken as the implication relation. What will eventually decide for us what relation to take as implication will be the results in practice of accepting one or the other. Ultimately, he thought, our conception of logical implication—as a relation that must obtain between statements that warrants inference from one to another— will be based on pragmatic grounds.

Other logicians, feeling that Lewis' account of implication fails to bring out features of the ordinary notion, have proposed alternatives. While none have been widely adopted by logicians, it remains to be seen whether any logical systems constructed with inference rules alternative to the standard systems will come to have a wide popularity.[7] Before we drop the subject of implication, however, a few further points require clarification.

c. Implication, Deducibility, and Meaning

As we have seen, C. I. Lewis explicated implication as the converse of the relation 'is deducible from'. At times he wrote of '*A* implies *B*' and '*B* is deducible from *A*' as "synonymous" expressions,[8] while at other times he wrote of them as "equivalent." [9] Lewis recognized that there is a sense in which 'implies', as he defined it, should *not* be identified with the converse of the deducibility relation. In addition, certain discoveries, of which Lewis could not be aware, have led many contemporary logicians to reject the identification. We can bring out some important points about the nature of deduction and implication by considering these arguments.

Let us suppose that a statement *A* implies a statement *B*. Now consider the argument that can be constructed having *A* as its premise and *B* as its conclusion. We have already shown that an argument is valid if, and only if, its premises imply its conclusion. Suppose *A* and *B* are both logically true statements. Then *A* implies *B,* and the argument with *A* as premise and *B* as conclusion is valid. As previously pointed out, however, we do not give a good argument to establish a logical truth merely by giving premises that logically imply that statement. The absurdity of such an attempt is easily shown. Consider the following statement-schema:

$$(A \supset (A \supset (B \lor (C \supset A))))$$

To a beginning student it probably is not obvious that any sentence having that form is logically true. Such a student would not be shown that this *is* a schema for logically true sentences, by being presented the following argument, even though it *is* a valid argument-form:

$$\frac{D}{(A \supset (A \supset (B \lor (C \supset A))))}$$

The example shows (at least) that we cannot suppose that if *A* implies *B*, then that is sufficient to conclude that the argument with *A* as premise, *B* as conclusion, is a *deduction* (in an ordinary sense of the word) of *B* from *A*.

Now, Lewis recognized this point (although he expressed it in a different, somewhat confusing way). He pointed out that if we make this mistake, we shall be led to the obviously erroneous conclusion that the entirety of the theorems of a logical system can be deduced from any assumptions at all. No one supposes this in practice, and considerable ingenuity is required to devise axiom systems and proofs that can be utilized to establish the theorems of logic. Lewis' explanation of this is interesting and important. In the next few paragraphs I shall sketch some of his central points (though Lewis expressed them differently).

Inference in a deductive system is always done according to rules. We start with axioms, and the rules tell us what further lines can be written down. All theorems are either axioms or derived from the axioms *according to the rules given or previously derived.* Thus, we cannot give a derivation of a theorem in a system *merely* by writing an argument with an arbitrarily selected premise and the theorem as conclusion. Of course, we *could* adopt the following rule of inference:

$$\left.\begin{array}{c} A \\ \hline B \end{array}\right\} \text{(where } A \text{ is any sentence and } B \text{ is any theorem)}$$

We could apply such a rule, however, *only* if *B* were already a theorem, in which case the inquiring student could always be directed to its proof.

In addition, Lewis pointed out that if the logical system is incomplete—has insufficient axioms or rules of inference—there will necessarily be some theorems that *cannot* be deduced in that system. Thus, there will be some logical truths that will not *be* theorems and that could never be "proved" by use of the rules. The upshot is that when he took '*A* implies *B*' as equivalent to '*B* is deducible from *A*', he did *not* mean that if *A* implies *B*, then '*A*, therefore *B*' *is* a deduction of *B* from *A*. Rather, he meant that there *are* valid patterns of inference whereby *B* *can* be deduced from *A*—i.e., that it is *possible* to deduce *B* from *A* using *some* acceptable inference rules. His "proof" that any statement can be deduced from a logically false statement was just such a demonstration; he produced rules of inference that he believed our logical intuitions would endorse as obviously valid, and he then showed how to make the derivation using them. Having shown that any statement can be derived from a logically false statement, he concluded that a logically false statement implies any statement.

Two further points concerning implication and deducibility must be mentioned. We have seen that logicians who accept our definition of 'implication' hold that *A* implies *B* if, and only if, '*A*, therefore *B*' is a valid argument. Lewis appears also to have accepted this. However, we have also argued that not every valid argument (in this sense) demonstrates its conclusion or counts as a derivation of the conclusion from the premises. What counts as a derivation depends on what rules of inference one can take to have available to begin with. We have demonstrated to an inquirer the implication of *B* by *A* only when we have derived *B* from *A* using rules of inference he already accepts, or which have been shown reliable. Within a deductive system, of course, the notion of a derivation is independent of anyone's beliefs, acceptances, and so on. Still, there is a distinction to be made between arguments that are valid and those that not only are valid but also *demonstrate* their conclusions. Whether or not one accepts the usual definitions of 'implication' and 'validity', it is important to be able to make out this distinction and give an account of it.[10]

The final point concerning implication and deducibility has been alluded to earlier. Lewis thought that a statement, *A*, implies a statement, *B*, if, and only if, *B* is deducible from *A*. Now, I think it is universally accepted that if *B* can be deduced from *A* by acceptable inference rules, then *A* implies *B*. But recent metalogical research (not known to Lewis) has led many logicians to deny that if *A* implies *B*, then there necessarily is a derivation of *B* from *A*. Kurt Gödel has shown, as we have noted,[11] that there can be no consistent axiom system for arithmetic that is complete. This means that there can be no consistent axiom system from which every theorem of arithmetic can be derived. Given our definition of 'implies', every axiom system is such that there will be some theorem or other that the axioms imply—it would not be possible for the axioms to be true and the theorem to be false—but there can be no deduction of that theorem from those axioms. Gödel's proof shows this will be true for any axiom system for arithmetic. For this reason many logicians reject the claim that implication is the converse of deducibility.[12]

The final claim to be discussed in this section is that implication is a meaning relation—i.e., that a statement, *A*, implies *B* if, and only if, the meaning of *A* includes or "contains" the meaning of *B*. What prompts this view is the thought that a statement can imply another if, and only if, there is some *relevance* between them; the one must "make" the other true. It is this lack that the supposedly paradoxical laws of strict implication reveal, since a logically false statement implies every statement merely by *its* being logically false, independent of any connection with the statements it strictly implies. Similarly, a logically true statement is strictly implied by any statement, however irrelevant to it that statement may be. The requirement that there be a connection of relevance between statements that stand in an implication relation has intuitive attractiveness and has been thought satisfied by insisting that there be a connection between the meanings of the sentences before an entailment relation holds. Grounds have been offered for denying that strict implication *fails* to meet the relevance test, and there are grounds for doubting that a meaning relation is either a necessary or sufficient condition for implication.

It is important to notice (some philosophers think) that the "paradoxes" arise with respect to logically false and logically true statements. These are strange creatures in ordinary discourse, and the fact that we get unintuitive results with our definition of 'implies' where statements of *these* kinds are involved can hardly show that the definition is counter-intuitive.[13] Moreover, why should we not conclude that Lewis' arguments show that a logical falsehood *is* "relevant" to every statement and every statement is "relevant" to a logical truth? Why not conclude that Lewis' proofs show that if a logically false statement is asserted, then there are no grounds for ruling out any statement ("If *that* were true, *anything* would be"), and that any statement is ground for a logically true statement ("*That* is true if anything is"). At the very least, the proofs do show there *is* some connection between every statement and a logical truth or falsehood—viz., a necessary connection of possible truth-values. Why the relevance criterion seems to fail is that we can determine the implication relationship merely in terms of the logical properties of the logical truth or logical falsehood alone. But why *couldn't* the possession of these (unusual) properties make a statement relevant to all statements? To rule out such a position would require a specification of 'relevance' and an explanation of why one statement cannot be relevant to another merely on the basis of properties possessed by the first alone.

Moreover, some simple considerations seem to show that a meaning relation is neither necessary nor sufficient for implication.[14] Let us take the second case first—a meaning relation is not a sufficient condition. Suppose I walk into a room that has three chairs in it and I say, 'There are three chairs in this room'. Then I go into a room that has no chairs and I say, 'There are three chairs in this room'. Now, the sentences I uttered were identical in meaning (the words 'this room' do not change *meaning* from room to room, even if they do change *referent*). Yet, what I said the first time was true, while what I said the second time was false. There is identity of meaning, but no implication.

Similar considerations (which involve distinguishing *meaning* from *reference*) show that a meaning relation is not a necessary condition for implication. Suppose John is 25 years old and lives in Berkeley, California, and Bill and I are discussing John while sitting in Berkeley. Bill says, 'John lives here and is 25 years old'. I conclude: 'Oh, then he lives in Berkeley'. What Bill said surely implied my conclusion, but the sentences uttered hardly have the same meaning; 'he' is not synonymous with 'John' and 'here' is not synonymous with 'Berkeley'. Without a clarification of the notion of "meaning containment," we have no ground for claiming that the meaning of the one statement contains that of the other. There can be little doubt, however, that the one implies the other.

Perhaps there is a theory of meaning that resolves these difficulties. If so, it would illuminate a host of other problems in the philosophy of logic. In the next section we shall take up a long-standing philosophical distinction, widely utilized in philosophy, that has been thought especially relevant to explaining the nature of logical truth. It has also been thought important in dealing with certain kinds of arguments, the validity of which seems to depend on relations of meaning between terms in the arguments. The distinction has become quite controversial among contemporary logicians and philosophers.

2. THE ANALYTIC-SYNTHETIC DISTINCTION

Consider the following argument:

> All men with legally dependent children are eligible for dependents insurance.
> All fathers in the philosophy department have legally dependent children.
> Therefore, all fathers in the philosophy department are eligible for dependents insurance.

The argument is undoubtedly valid. However, if we seek to set out its form, there is no straightforward way to do so that reflects its validity. The reason is that the initial premise contains the term 'men', while the conclusion has 'fathers'. What relates the premise to the conclusion is not a *formal* characteristic but the fact that all fathers are men. Now, what sort of statement is 'all fathers are men'?

To many philosophers, statements of this kind have seemed to be like logical truths in that they are necessarily true. In this case the necessity is guaranteed not by the *form* of the statement but by virtue of the meanings of the terms. A statement that is true merely by virtue of the meanings of the terms requires nothing beyond itself to be true; hence, it could not be falsified by any fact about the world. If we can add statements of this kind to our deductive apparatus, we will have a tool for handling arguments such as the one above. The addition of the statement 'all fathers are men' to the premises of our argument would result in an argument that could be shown formally valid. Statements of this kind have been called *analytic,* and they have been contrasted with statements that cannot be denominated true (or false) merely by appeal to the meanings of the words but that depend on some further fact about reality; these latter are called *synthetic* statements. An example would be 'All fathers in the philosophy department are blond-haired'. We cannot determine its truth or falsity merely by knowing the meanings of the words. Thus, it has been thought that a sharp distinction can be drawn among statements according to whether they are analytic or synthetic.

Similar distinctions were made by the historically important philosophers Gottfried Leibniz, David Hume, and Immanuel Kant. In one form or another the distinction has been used within philosophy quite widely and by diverse schools. It is connected with important philosophical doctrines. In recent years, however, it has become quite controversial, and some contemporary philosophers deny that any such distinction can be intelligibly made. It is not possible to survey the various positions taken on the issue. In this section we can only sketch some of the ways in which the distinction has been stated and some of the most crucial objections that have launched the controversy.

The most influential statement of the distinction is found in the work of the philosopher Immanuel Kant.[15] Kant's distinction between the analytic and the synthetic was a central part of his theory of knowledge and must be understood in connection with a further distinction he made between a priori and a posteriori truths. A priori truths can be known true prior to experience—or, more precisely: *a priori* truths do not require our learning some fact through experience to know they are true. *A posteriori* truths do require confirmation in experience. The distinction is sometimes hard for students to grasp because an a priori truth may contain concepts that are acquired through experience. For example, it may be that a person who was blind from birth could not have the concept of colors and, in particular, of redness. These may be concepts one can acquire only through experience. Once one has these concepts, however, he or she needs no further experience in order to know that the statement 'All red things are colored' is true. In contrast, one could not know that the statement 'All the marbles in my pocket are red' is true without looking or discovering in experience evidence for its truth. All a priori judgments contain the notion of "strict universality"—i.e., are true of all things of a kind whether previously observed or not—and the notion of necessity—that those things *could not* be otherwise. Neither of these concepts is found in experience. Kant gave as an example, "Every change must have a cause." The distinction between a priori and a posteriori truths was based on different ways in which statements can be *known* to be true.

The analytic-synthetic distinction was made by Kant as follows. Analytic statements are such that the subject contains the predicate; i.e., the predicate adds nothing that is not already within the conception of the subject. An example might be 'All fathers are men'. Synthetic statements, on the other hand, are such that the predicate adds something not already part of the conception of the subject. In 'All fathers have two kidneys' we do have in the predicate something not already part of the subject; the concept of being a father does not (it would seem) include (or exclude) the idea of having two kidneys. Kant distinguished between analytic and synthetic statements on the basis of relations between the components of the statements, not on the basis of how they are known.

Of very great importance in the subsequent history of philosophy has been the question of possible combinations among the designations 'a priori', 'a posteriori', 'analytic', 'synthetic'.

It is fairly clear that all analytic statements are a priori and none are a posteriori. A statement in which the predicate merely repeats part of what is conveyed in the subect requires no experience as evidence that it is true. But Kant maintains that some statements are both synthetic and a priori. The statement '7 + 5 = 12' is not analytic, he thought, since the idea or concept of adding 7 and 5 does not contain the idea of 12. Moreover, it is not a posteriori, since it requires no experience to be known true; it does not "depend on" experience. Kant thought of all mathematics as expressing synthetic a priori statements; moreover, he thought the causal maxim 'Everything that happens has a cause' is a synthetic a priori statement. Indeed, he thought that basic to all science and mathematics are synthetic a priori principles. His work in the theory of knowledge was directed at determining how such principles are possible. His conclusion, put quite succinctly, was that the mind is so constituted that it necessarily organizes experience through or by means of certain a priori concepts or categories. Without having in thought concepts such as space, time, causality, and so on, we would not experience objects, only a flow of sensations. The a priori concepts are contributed by the mind.

The issues in the theory of knowledge that Kant's claims raise are beyond our concerns. Those views have been mentioned to provide a further perspective within which the analytic-synthetic distinction can be placed. It has become much more common in recent years for philosophers to regard all a priori statements as analytic, though Kant's view continues to have its adherents. Our concern is with the analytic-synthetic distinction, insofar as that bears on the validity of certain kinds of arguments.

Kant distinguished analytic from synthetic statements in terms of the inclusion of one concept by another—the inclusion of the concept of the predicate by the subject. This has seemed unsatisfactory to many philosophers, since we need criteria for saying when we have identical or different concepts and when one concept includes another. In its more contemporary formulation the problem has been posed as that of saying when two expressions *have the same meaning* or are *synonymous*. The leading critic of attempts to explicate these notions has been Willard Van Orman Quine.[16] We shall briefly indicate some of the difficulties.

First of all, it is very important to distinguish between the meaning or sense of an expression and its referent, the thing or things it applies to or is true of. This was shown clearly in the last century by Gottlob Frege,[17] an important German logician. The example he used is so apt, it is widely used even today. Consider the expressions 'the Evening Star' and 'the Morning Star'. The first came to be used for an object that appears very bright at certain times of the year in the evening. The second came to be used for a bright object that appears on the horizon in the morning. Astronomers made the discovery that, in fact, this was the same object—the planet Venus. Though they have the same referent, the expressions 'the Morning Star' and 'the Evening Star' differ in sense or meaning. Meaning is *not* to be explicated, then, in terms of the things referred to.

Another way in which to explain analytic statements is to claim they are true *by definition*. Now, this helps a little, for we know where to look to find definitions—in the dictionary. But, as Quine points out, the dictionary is a report on usage; it represents the dictionary maker's judgment that certain terms are so used as to be synonymous. But then, the appeal to definitions rests ultimately on an unanalyzed notion of synonymous expressions. It is that concept for which we were seeking an explanation in the first place.

One promising thought has been that terms that are synonymous can be exchanged for one another in sentences without changing the truth-values of the sentences. So, if a true sentence contains 'male parent', we should be able to substitute 'father' for the longer expression and the statement will remain true. Consider the following sentences, however:

(1)   Necessarily all fathers are fathers.
(2)   Necessarily all fathers are male parents.

Here, we seem to preserve truth-value despite an exchange of one term for another. The criterion seems to work. But in virtue of what knowledge do we claim (2) to be true? Have we not implicitly supposed the necessity to derive from the fact that the following statement is analytic:

(3)   All fathers are male parents.

In that case, however, the entire process rests on our understanding analyticity independently of the notion of interchangeability. Though the criterion works, it presupposes the very thing it was to help explain; we cannot apply the criterion unless we can tell which statements are analytic, else we shall not be able to affirm *that* the criterion works in contexts such as those in (1) and (2) above.[18]

Despite attacks such as these by Quine and others, the analytic-synthetic distinction continues to enjoy wide adherence. Various attempts have been made to defend it among philosophers and philosophically minded linguists.[19] It has been a useful tool in dealing with particular philosophical problems. One's view of the distinction itself, however, is intimately connected with one's conception of the nature of logic, knowledge, and reality. Quine's rejection of the distinction is tied up, for example, with his view that all truths must meet the test of experience and have both linguistic and extralinguistic aspects.[20]

Because the issues are so important, we have barely scratched the surface of the debate that has taken place over the analytic-synthetic distinction. Our purpose has been merely to expose the student to the problem and to some of the positions that have been taken with respect to it. We shall go on to consider another problem that concerns logicians and that has also been thought to be resolved by appeal to meanings.

3. SENTENCES AND PROPOSITIONS

The logician is intimately concerned with validity. Validity has been explicated in terms of a necessary connection among truth-values of statements. But our term 'statement' has been purposely employed in an ambiguous way to mask a problem that has vexed philosophers. This problem can be posed as a question: what *is* it that has a truth-value; what is it that is true or false? Well, if anything is true or false, statements are. But what, exactly, is a statement? The answers to this question have differed greatly. Put in a somewhat uninformative way: a statement is what someone says, expresses, or asserts when he or she says something that is true or false. But what *is* it that can be said, expressed, asserted, and that can be true or false? Let us consider several answers.

First, it is sometimes contended that what is true or false are *sentences*. This answer seems unsatisfactory to many logicians, because it seems that one can say, express, or assert the same thing using different sentences. Consider the following list:

(1) I have it.
(2) Yo lo tengo.
(3) Ich habe das.
(4) Jeg har det.
(5) Yes. (Said in answer to the question: Do you have it?)

In appropriate contexts, each of these sentences can be used to assert the same thing. (2), (3), and (4) say in Spanish, German, and Norwegian what is said using the English sentences in (1) and (5). Not only can we assert the same thing in different languages (thus using different sentences), but we can assert the same thing in the same language with different sentences. But if we have asserted the same thing, and the sentences uttered are different, then the sentences cannot be what we asserted.

The claim for sentences is even more unstable. Consider the sentence 'There are three books in this room now'. If I utter this in appropriate circumstances, and there are three books in the room in which I am located, then I shall have said something true. If I utter the same sentence, however, in an adjoining room that has no books in it, I shall have said something false. Now, if what is asserted in each case is the sentence uttered, then, since the same sentence is uttered, I shall have asserted something that is both true and false. Obviously, to take statements as sentences would create substantial difficulties.

We have, however, ignored a certain ambiguity in the notion of a sentence. Sentences are composed of words, themselves made up of letters (when written); sentences can be uttered, written on paper, chalked on a blackboard, and so on. What is it, however, that one puts on a blackboard? Chalk marks that have recognizable configurations. Is *that* the sentence? In one sense it undoubtedly is. We can speak of pointing to the sentence on the blackboard, and presumably what can be pointed to occupies space. On the other hand, we also say we can write the same sentence again on the blackboard *or* on a piece of paper. But in that case we do not mean by 'sentence' the chalk marks on the blackboard. When we write the same sentence on a piece of paper, we do not transfer those chalk marks to the paper. Indeed, even if we wrote the sentence on the paper with chalk, *those* would be a different set of marks from the ones on the board.

Logicians mark this distinction by speaking of different "instances" or "occurrences" of the same sentence. Each instance is said to be a *token* of a sentence-*type*. (The distinction is due to the American logician Charles Sanders Peirce, whose work is discussed in Chapter IV.)

In our arguments concerning sentences we have assumed we were speaking of sentence-types, for only in that sense could one be said to utter the same sentence in two different rooms at two different times. Moreover, sentence-tokens are not really candidates at all to fill the role of what (1)–(5) are all used to assert. In each case *different* tokens are employed; that is part of how the problem got started. Indeed, it would become impossible in most contexts to say the same thing more than once, even by using the same sentence-type. Once we have made particular sounds, *those* particular ones are gone forever. Of course, written tokens could sometimes be reused—e.g., by cutting them out of a particular discourse and pasting them in another. But surely this is to make nonsense of the notion of saying the same thing on more than one occasion.

Professor Quine has suggested (in fact, has maintained) that it is a particular *utterance* that is true or false.[21] An utterance (in this sense) is an event that takes place in writing or in the uttering of appropriate words. But it seems to strain the bounds of sense to speak of *events* as true or false. Moreover, the suggestion seems to fuse two very different things: the event in which something is asserted and that which is asserted *in* that event. Of course, Quine is probably under no illusions on this score. He holds also that sentence-tokens can, in a derivative way, be regarded as true or false relative to the circumstances of their utterance. And he holds that "eternal" sentences—ones such as in mathematics—are always true or false.

Historically, there have been many candidates for the role we are considering. The various sentences in our list can be said to express the same *thought, idea, judgment,* or *meaning*. These have been taken as mental entities or, on the other hand, as abstract entities—things that exist apart from mental or physical things. As psychological theories of meaning no longer have great popularity among philosophers, the prime candidate in recent years for the role of bearers of truth-value have been the meanings of sentences. The meanings of sentences are said to be *propositions;* thus, the list (1)–(5) are all said to express the same proposition. It is propositions in this sense—as the meanings of sentences—that philosophers such as Quine have been arguing against. Suppose we agree to call what each of (1)–(5) asserts or states a proposition. Merely saying this does not commit us to taking propositions to be the meanings of sentences. We can then go on to ask whether propositions are to be identified as the meanings of sentences.

Quine's arguments against propositions are easily misunderstood. His objection is not an objection to abstract entities as such. He is willing to assert the existence of sets in mathematics that are as abstract as entities get. Moreover, he thinks that in a derivative way "eternal" sentences, abstracted from events of utterance, can be said to be true or false. These are always true or false and are sentence-*types*. Rather, his objections are related to his objections to the analytic-synthetic distinction. If propositions are the meanings of sentences, then saying two sentences express the same proposition just means that they have the same meaning. But, specifying criteria for synonymy of sentence meaning is at least as difficult as specifying such criteria for terms. The problem, as he sees it, is not that meanings are abstract entities, but, rather, that there are no criteria for individuating them—i.e., for saying when given sentences have the same or different meanings. Since he also believes there is no useful purpose served in accepting them, he rejects them.[22]

The rejection of propositions as the meanings of sentences need not be based on acceptance of Quine's views concerning synonymity. Consider sentences (1) and (5) on our list above. Each can be used to assert the same proposition, but it is hardly plausible to hold that the words 'I have it' and 'Yes' have the same meaning. While the meanings we ascribe to words used on an occasion may depend on the context of the utterance, we would not be led to ascribe the same meanings to *those* words, owing to the understood contexts. Consider, further, the sentence 'It's raining'. What is *said* each time these words are uttered depends on the context. If I assert this on January 3, 1976, in New York City, what I say—the proposition expressed—will be true if, and only if, rain is falling in New York City on that day. If I say 'It's raining' on January 5, 1976, in Miami, what I say—the proposition expressed—will be true if, and only if, it is raining in Miami that day, regardless of the state of the weather in New York on January 3. So, different propositions are expressed. But the meanings of the words do not change every day and with every change of place. Indeed, it would seem that we *can* tell from the context what is asserted each time only because the *meanings* of the words do *not* change.

Finally, it has been argued that meanings do not have the right properties to take the role of that which is asserted when we say something that is true or false. For one thing, it is not clear that meanings can be true or false. Nor would it seem that a meaning could be silly, absurd, improbable, and so on, whereas what someone asserted can be all of these. Of course, if we had a theory of what meanings are, and what sentence meanings, in particular, are, that met all the other needs of a theory of meaning, we might come to find it sensible to attribute these properties to meanings. Even so, some philosophers have thought that the absurdity of such attributions rules out the very possibility of a theory of meaning that identifies propositions with the meanings of sentences.

One last view to be mentioned is that of Richard Gale, sketched in the *Encyclopedia of Philosophy*.[23] Gale agrees with the critics of the view that what is true or false is a sentence-token or an utterance of one. On the other hand, he thinks those philosophers who take propositions to be abstract entities are misled by the grammar of such expressions as 'says', 'states', 'asserts'. The mistake comes in supposing that such accusative verbs indicate a relation between two things or objects. Accusative verbs sometimes *do* indicate a relation between two things—e.g., 'hit', 'threw', 'ran into'. This is not always the case. To use one of Gale's examples, someone can dance the waltz without our having to suppose that the waltz is some "thing" that exists apart from the dancing. Even though things that are true of the dancing are not true of the waltz (as was the case with someone's saying something and what he said); nonetheless, we are not led to suppose there are two different things or objects. It is Gale's contention that verbs such as 'states', 'says' are unlike verbs such as 'hit', 'throws', and so on; they do not signify a relation between two objects. There are only acts of utterance, and what is said is a conceptually identifiable aspect of that event. The proposition does not exist apart from the act of utterance. (or conceptual entertainments?)

This, of course, is an outline of a view, not an argument for it. It needs to be shown that verbs such as 'says', 'states', 'asserts' have or lack the logical features Gale claims. As many philosophers have thought that there are many things that have never been asserted or stated, an *argument* is needed to show either that such claims are false or that they are properly understood in such a way that they do not imply the existence of anything apart from acts of utterance. (Are there also plays and poems that have never been written, symphonies that have never been composed? How many are there? How would one identify them?)

The most serious point to be made about the proposal, however, is that while it would rule out a certain metaphysical view concerning the status in reality of propositions, it still provides no criteria for individuating propositions. We still would not know how to tell when the same proposition is to be identified in two different speech acts.

It would seem, then, that if a theory of propositions, as different from sentences, is to be maintained, it will rest eventually on a broad theory of language that can provide clear criteria for identifying and individuating the various elements of those events that consist of someone's saying something that is true or false. At least it is clear that a great many philosophers and logicians will not be satisfied with a theory of propositions until such a general theory of language has been developed that is acceptable to them.

Next we shall consider a series of problems that relate in a broad way to the issues of this section.

4. PROPOSITIONAL ATTITUDES, INTENSIONS, AND MODES: EPISTEMIC, MODAL, AND DEONTIC LOGIC

In the preceding section we developed certain views about propositions by concentrating on features of such verbs as 'says', 'states', 'asserts'. One way of interpreting their function is to hold that they indicate an attitude toward something—a proposition. To assert or state something is to endorse it as true. Other verbs also indicate a stance toward propositions. We can question, doubt, think, know that something is true. Each of these verbs can be interpreted as indicating an attitude toward what can be asserted as true or false. As it is propositions toward which these attitudes are supposedly taken, these verbs are sometimes called verbs of *propositional attitude*. A further terminology for them derives from a long-standing philosophical distinction.

In the 1600's, philosophers distinguished the *extension* of a term from its *comprehension*. The extension is the class of things to which the term applies; the comprehension is the set of properties in virtue of which the term is applied to them, or, in the older way of putting it: it is those characteristics which, if taken away, would destroy the idea. In later years the comprehension of a term has been called its *intension,* and intensions are thought to be meanings.[24] (The student should note the difference in spelling between 'intensions' and 'intentions'. It is hard to state clearly what relation there is between their meanings.) The upshot is that verbs of propositional attitude are said to have intensions as objects, and the logic that deals with arguments in which such verbs occur in an essential way is called *intensional logic.* Another basis for this classification, which is more crucial in certain respects, will be explored later.

We turn now to elucidating features of arguments containing the verbs of propositional attitude; we shall see why some logicians have thought a special kind of logic must be devised for them. Consider the following arguments:

> John believes that Smith is the mailman.
> The mailman is John's wife's lover.
> John believes that Smith is John's wife's lover.

> John doubts that Smith is John's wife's lover.
> Smith is the mailman.
> John doubts that Smith is the mailman.

> John knows that Mary is John's wife.
> John's wife is the lady having an affair with Smith.
> John knows that Mary is the lady having an affair with Smith.

In each of these arguments is a premise that can be taken to have the form:

$$(a = b)$$

For example, in the first argument we get the second statement if we replace '*a*' in the above form with 'The mailman' and '*b*' with 'John's wife's lover', and if we regard '=' as an abbreviation or replacement for 'is'. Now, the following has seemed to many to be obviously true:

> Of any objects *a* and *b*, if ($a = b$), then anything true of *a* is true of *b* and vice versa.

Indeed, this is a theorem of standard identity logic, symbolized as:

$$(x)(y)((x = y) \supset (Fx \equiv Fy)).$$

It has been dubbed the Principle of the Indiscernibility of Identicals [25] [if ($a = b$), then *a* and *b* are indiscernible]. One obvious way of interpreting this is to say that if ($a = b$), then in any sentence containing a term referring to *a*, a term referring to *b* can be put in its place without altering the truth-value of the sentence.[26] If the original sentence was true, then, necessarily, the new sentence will also be true; if the original was false, so will be the new sentence.

What gives this principle initial plausibility are the following considerations. If *a* and *b* are identical, then all that happens when we change the original sentence is that we replace one term that refers to *a* with *another* term that refers to *a*. The new term, to be sure, refers to *b*, but, since (*a* = *b*), the new term refers to *a*. We have merely changed the *way* in which we have referred to *a*. But the manner in which we refer to an object should not change the truth or falsity of what we say of it. If John's wife is an adultress, then she is such whether we refer to her using 'John's wife', 'Smith's mistress', 'Kowalski's daughter', or 'the lady in the polka-dot dress'. We cannot alter the modes in which she has found her pleasures merely by changing the manner in which we refer to her.

Compelling as such considerations may be, our sample arguments show that the principle cannot be applied without restriction when the sentences involved contain verbs of propositional attitude. Consider the first argument. The second premise, together with the principle of the indiscernibility of identicals (interpreted as permitting substitutivity of terms), would warrant transforming the first premise into the conclusion. If such transformation is thought always to preserve truth-value, then we shall be forced to regard the conclusion as true if the premises are true. In other words, we shall be forced to regard the argument as valid. It clearly is not valid, however.

The reasons why none of our sample arguments is valid are not hard to find. Beginning students can pick them out. If we look again at the first argument, we can readily see that it is possible for the premises to be true and the conclusion false. Supposing John and his wife to have a conventional marriage and supposing his wife to have been successfully secretive about the love affair she is having, it might well be true that Smith is John's wife's lover and that John is acquainted with Smith as the mailman. But he may have no inkling that Smith is his wife's lover. He may, for example, feel sure she is seeing the next-door neighbor. Knowing Smith *as the mailman* does not entail knowing all of his identifications. Believing someone to have a certain property that he does have need not entail believing him to have other properties he does have. The propositional attitudes involved are directed at certain of the identifications of the object and not at others. Or, put somewhat more clearly: in linguistic contexts introduced by such terms as 'knows', 'believes', 'doubts', and so on, referring expressions function as more than mere references to objects; they also indicate the object *in a particular way*.

There is something else important about these considerations. Our rejection of the validity of the three sample arguments was based on an understanding of the meaning and force of the expressions 'knows', 'believes', 'doubts'. We could have taken those arguments and treated them as we did arguments in Chapter I; i.e., we could have constructed a form for each argument that would contain the expressions 'knows', 'believes', 'doubts', and no other expressions except logical constants. For example, we could represent the form of the first argument as follows:

> A believes that $(b = c)$.
> $(c = d)$.
> _____
> A believes that $(b = d)$.

Our argument concerning the way 'believes that' functions could as well have been directed at this argument-form. Now this sort of feature, we saw, characterizes logical constants. It is on the basis of appeal to *their* meanings in argument-forms that we are able to establish that substitution-instances of those forms are valid or not. The concepts of knowledge and belief are of central importance in the theory of knowledge. For reasons such as these, philosophers have been led to develop logical systems containing expressions of propositional attitude that are treated as logical constants. These systems can be used to test the validity of arguments utilizing such expressions. The branch of philosophy that attempts to explain knowledge and belief is called *epistemology,* and this new branch of logic is called *epistemic* logic.

We pointed out earlier that epistemic logic is said to be a kind of "intensional" logic, insofar as the objects of propositional attitudes are said to be intensions. There is, in fact, a wider usage of the term 'intensional logic', which does not involve propositional attitudes. This usage turns on the fact that there are a number of kinds of linguistic context in which referring expressions are not "purely referential" (as Quine has put it).[27]

Our main clue that the referring expressions in our sample arguments do not function merely to indicate objects was that the sentences in which they occur could change truth-value if other expressions referring to the same objects were substituted. We can attribute this to the introduction of the epistemic terms 'knows' and 'believes', partly because our argument for the invalidity of the samples appeals to the meanings of those terms and also because the referring expression preceding the introduction of those term *does* permit substitution without change of truth-value. *Any* expression referring to John (so long as *it* does not contain an epistemic term, e.g., 'the man who believes that . . . ') can be put in for his name without altering the truth-value the original sentence had. In contemporary usage, any context in which substitutivity fails is called an *intensional* context (other names: *indirect* context, *opaque* context, *oblique* context, *nonextensional* context).

Other expressions that philosophers have thought important also introduce intensional contexts. The most important are the expressions 'necessarily' and 'possibly'. These are not verbs of propositional attitude; rather, they indicate the "manner" or "mode" of truth or falsity of a statement—whether it is necessarily or possibly true or false. Systems of logic that seek to deal with arguments containing these terms are called *modal* logics. We can show that these expressions introduce intensional contexts. Consider the following argument:

> Necessarily, 30 is less than 40.
> The number of students in Mary's logic class is 30.
> ———————————————————————————
> Necessarily, the number of students in Mary's logic class is less than 40.

Should this seem to be a valid argument, the student should note the conclusion's assertion that it is *necessarily* the case that Mary's logic class has fewer than 40 students. But that means there could not possibly have been 45, or 50, or 100 students in the class. The number of students in a logic class, however, seems subject to numerous contingencies—e.g., what time of day it is given, what courses it competes with, the text being used, whether or not the course has been required by some department, and so on. The last-mentioned contingency could easily result in a large enrollment, and so it is possible for Mary's class to have a larger enrollment than 40 students.[28] So the conclusion of the above argument is false, even if the premises are true. Thus, the argument is invalid. The conclusion, however, is merely the result of substituting one expression for another that refers to the same thing. The adverb, 'necessarily', then, introduces an intensional context.

Again, philosophers have thought the concepts of necessity and possibility to be extremely important. Our definition of 'logically implies' involves these concepts. Consequently, it has seemed important to many philosophers and logicians to seek to develop logical systems for arguments in which these terms occur. As these expressions indicate the mode of the truth or falsity of statements, these logical systems are called *modal* logics.

A further kind of logical system can be thought of as modal. The sort of logic I am speaking of is called *deontic* logic. It employs as special logical constants expressions interpreted as 'it is permissible that', 'it is obligatory that', 'it is forbidden that'. Such expressions indicate the manner or mode in which an act stands from the point of view of some set of normative standards. Certain earlier logicians treated the logic of modality in a broad way that would include any sort of adverbial qualification, and the normative modes were among them.[29]

These three kinds of logical systems—epistemic, modal, and deontic —are highly controversial, and all are rejected by some logicians as not properly a part of logic. It is instructive to see some of the reasons for these negative views.

First, some logicians object to epistemic and modal logic *because* they are intensional logics. This means that these logics add to the symbolism utilized in basic logic further symbols interpreted in such a way that difficulties of the kinds already mentioned arise. These difficulties are of three kinds, and thus there are three ways in which a language (or logic expressed in a language) can be intensional.

The first kind of intensionality arises with respect to sentences that themselves contain sentences. Sentential logic was said to be truth-functional (in Chapter I) because all compound sentences were regarded as being entirely determined in truth-value by the component sentences. This means that if *A* is a part of a compound *B*, then if we replace *A* in the compound with any other sentence that has the same truth-value, the new compound will have the same truth-value as the old. Now, the verbs of propositional attitude and the modal expressions are written before sentences that are thus parts of a whole:

(1) John believes Mary is at home.
(2) Necessarily, Mary's logic class is overcrowded.

These sentences are not truth-functional. Suppose Mary is at home and so is Susan, but John thinks Susan is at work. If he believes Mary is at home, then (1) is true. But, if we substitute 'Susan is at home' for 'Mary is at home' in (1), the result will be false. With respect to (2), though Mary's logic class *is* overcrowded, this is not necessarily true, so (2) is false. If we put '2 + 2 = 4' for 'Mary's logic class is overcrowded', we get

(3) Necessarily, 2 + 2 = 4.

Whereas (2) is false, (3) is true even though (3) is merely the result of replacing a component sentence of (2) with another that has the same truth-value. So, we can say that epistemic and modal logics are intensional with respect to *sentence-substitution*.

The second sort of intensionality can be illustrated in the following way. Suppose a new philosophy department at a certain college, A.S.U., graduates its first two Ph.D.'s, both of whom become members of the department at another school, C.S.U. Suppose also that they are the only members. Thus, the following will be true:

(1) All Ph.D.'s from A.S.U. are members of the department at C.S.U.

and:

(2)   All members of the department at C.S.U. are Ph.D.'s from A.S.U.

Now, two predicates are said to *have the same extension* if, and only if, they truly apply to the same class of objects. Since (1) and (2) are true, the predicates 'is a Ph.D. from A.S.U.' and 'is a member of the department at C.S.U.' have the same extension. A language can be said to be intensional with respect to *predicate-substitution* if it is possible for sentences to change in truth-value if predicates having the same extension are substituted within them. Since someone could know (1) above without knowing (2), we can easily construct a sentence using 'knows that' that would not permit predicate-substitution. We shall not provide an example for modal terms, but they too fail to permit predicate-substitution without alteration of truth-value.

The last kind of intensionality—intensionality with respect to *reference-term-substitution*—we illustrated earlier and have been working with all along.

A language in which all three forms of substitutivity can be done *without* changing the truth-values of the sentences is said to be an *extensional* language. Obviously, a great advantage can be gained if logic can be developed so that it is adequate for the major purposes for which we want logic and its symbolism can be interpreted in such a way that it is extensional. Deduction in an extensional language is greatly simplified. Some philosophers, in fact, have thought that everything of importance we need to be able to say in science and mathematics can be expressed in an extensional language. This view was held by Bertrand Russell and argued for at one time by Rudolf Carnap, one of the leading lights of a school of philosophers known as *logical positivists*. The claim that this is true is known as the Thesis of Extensionality.[30] It is worth noting that Quine, who has been the foremost critic of intensional logics, does not go quite this far. Though he is unwilling to regard a science as finally developed if it employs intensional terms in irreducible ways, he does not hold that an extensional language is enough for science. In particular, he has expressed doubt that the verbs of propositional attitude can be dispensed with.[31] In addition, Carnap later came to deny the Thesis of Extensionality and became an important contributor to intensionalist semantics and to the development of modal logic.[32]

The second sort of objection that some philosophers have had to intensional logics, and to deontic logic also, arises from considerable puzzlement and disagreement over what to accept as theorems or truths of such systems. C. I. Lewis, one of the modern pioneers of modal logic, propounded five *different* systems. They can be arranged in ascending order in the following sense: the second contains all the theorems of the first, plus additional theorems; the third contains all the theorems of the second, plus additional theorems, and so on. Moreover, other systems have been proposed. This means that it is not always intuitively obvious what statements employing modal expressions are logically true. Consider whether you would be willing to adopt the following as logical truths:

If a statement *A* is possible, then *A* is necessarily possible.
If a statement *A* is necessary, then necessarily *A* is necessary.

Similar disagreement infects epistemic and deontic logic. In epistemic logic, for example, the following statements have been taken in some systems as logical truths and dropped in others:

If a person, *a*, knows that *A*, then *a* knows that *a* knows that *A*.
If a person, *a*, believes that *A*, then *a* knows that *a* believes that *A*.

Some philosophers think that these disagreements (along with further difficulties) show that we do not understand intensional terms very well, and that nothing but confusion results from their employment. Others have felt that the difficulties show that the development of these logics is itself dependent on philosophical clarification of the basic notions.

Finally, some logicians think of these fields as not logic at all. There are various grounds for such views. One, of some importance, turns on pointing out that if we accept such expressions as 'believes', 'necessarily', 'it is permissible that' into logic as logical constants, there can be no ground for excluding hosts of others, for virtually any expression can, in certain contexts, be crucial in determining the validity of arguments in which it occurs. Statements containing the term 'father' may be contained in arguments the validity of which can be ascertained by appeal to the meaning of 'father'.[33] Is there, then, a "logic" of fatherhood? The fear is that we are apt to lose the concept of a logical constant entirely if we go beyond the terms of basic logic to let in new logical constants.

Although these fields are controversial, there is great interest in them among contemporary logicians. Many feel that no apologies need be made for these systems. Historically speaking, all have credentials of long standing. Aristotle made contributions to modal logic alongside his development of traditional syllogistic logic, and basic theorems of epistemic logic have been debated informally for centuries. And, as we saw earlier, there has been a tradition that regards deontic logic as dealing with one among many modal logics.

In addition, it can be argued that virtually any expression *is* capable of functioning like a logical constant in the sense in which we have been using that term. The concept is one that is relative to a range of arguments; i.e., it is by virtue of the role of expressions such as 'if ___, then ___', 'or', 'all', and so on in a very wide range of arguments that we single them out as logical constants. In basic logic the range of arguments we can deal with is very great. But, it may be contended, the terms introduced into epistemic, modal, and deontic logic are important in a wide range of contexts also and in important areas of philosophical concern. This justifies giving explicit attention to them, especially as a great many philosophical difficulties have been thought to be illuminable by the development of these logics. Moreover, the philosophical discussion of such concepts as necessity, knowledge, belief, and obligation can be furthered by the attempt to deal with them with the techniques of contemporary logic. Philosophical investigation is not something to be done *independently* and beforehand. And, where there are divergent theories or alternative understandings of these notions, the attempt to systematize those theories and trace out their consequences can be a contribution to philosophical understanding. Whether one thinks of these studies as a part of logic proper, or as applications of logical techniques to fields outside of logic, the fact is that a great deal of work is being done in these areas by logicians.

In the next section we shall take up kinds of systems of logic that differ in a more radical way from standard, basic logic.

5. NONSTANDARD (DEVIANT) LOGICS

The various kinds of logical systems we have discussed so far in this chapter, with only one exception, may be regarded as extensions of basic logic. These systems do not reject any of the theorems of a standard logical system, nor do they reject as valid any arguments that are valid in basic logic. Rather, they are designed to deal with a wider range of arguments. They employ a new symbolism and add to the list of valid inference patterns argument-forms in which these new symbols occur. The one exception, of course, consists of that group of systems explicitly designed to capture an alternative sense of 'logical implication'. Such systems—which require that there be "relevance" of premises to conclusion —need not reject as true any theorems of standard logic; what is rejected is the claim that certain inferences are valid.[34]

In this section we shall briefly discuss approaches to logic that are like the "relevance" or "implicational" logics—they reject some aspect of standard logic. We shall consider a logic as *nonstandard* (also sometimes called *deviant*)[35] if it rejects either: (a) a presupposition of basic logic, (b) a theorem of basic logic, (c) an inference rule regarded as valid in basic logic. Quite clearly, a logic that met one of these conditions would be radically *different from* standard logic, not a mere supplement to it. Some examples of the sort of deviance we have in mind will illustrate the point. Standard logic presupposes the truth of the Principle of Bivalence:

Every statement is either true or false.

It also presupposes the truth of the Principle of Non-contradiction (or what might be called the Principle of Univalence):

No statement is both true and false.

Among logicians and logically minded philosophers, almost none have questioned the second principle, but the first—the Principle of Bivalence —has been questioned on various grounds, some of which we shall outline later. The point here is that a logical system that rejects the Principle of Bivalence must present an aspect radically different from standard logic. Insofar as a standard interpretation assigns either truth or falsity to every sentence, such a logic must differ from standard logic *at least* with respect to what it counts as an interpretation of its symbolism.

The second way in which a logic may differ from standard logic is in rejecting as a theorem of logic some sentence that is a theorem of standard logic. One prime candidate has been what is called the Law of Excluded Middle.[36]

$$(P \lor -P)$$

Indeed, the reasons that have been thought to count against the Principle of Bivalence have usually been thought to count against the Law of Excluded Middle.[37]

Finally, a logician may differ from the standard logician in what his system would certify as the set of valid arguments. As we have seen, the orthodox logician accepts as valid any argument having either of the following forms:

$$\frac{(A \& -A)}{B} \qquad \frac{B}{(A \lor -A)}$$

where *B* is any sentence at all. As this appears to violate the intuitive notion that sentences that entail one another must at least be relevant to one another, such arguments would not be certified as valid by logicians who adopt the alternative conception of implication.

Of course, deviance of one of these three kinds can lead to deviance of the other kinds. For example, if the Law of Excluded Middle is not a theorem in a logician's system, then arguments having the form

$$\frac{B}{(A \vee -A)}$$

may not be accepted as valid even if the standard definition of entailment is accepted.

The various alternative logics that have been proposed raise very difficult problems. For example, if a system does not contain one of the standard laws, it has been maintained that the logician proposing it has changed the meanings of the logical symbols. For example, if his system fails to count '$(P \vee -P)$' as a theorem, then he cannot be using '$\vee$' and '$-$' in the same senses these connectives have in standard logic. Hence, the new system does not deny anything the standard system asserts; it simply asserts different things. Given the *standard* meaning of '$(P \vee -P)$', this sentence is surely true; to (try to) say otherwise is really to reinterpret the connectives.[38]

In addition, it is sometimes difficult to tell when a so-called "alternative" really *is* alternative. For example, it has been proposed that there are really three truth-values: true, false, and possible. In accord with the suggestion, a three-valued logic has been proposed and defended. On the other hand, it has been argued that the system, especially in light of the informal explanations given it, permits interpreting sentences as not having *truth*-values but *certainty*-values; i.e., of every statement, A, we can say either:

It is certain that A.

or

It is not certain that A and it is not certain that $-A$.

or

It is certain that $-A$.

What I have called *certainty-values* clearly presuppose the ordinary truth-values. Every statement *is* either true or false; it is simply that we are uncertain as to which. So, it has been argued this proposed "alternative" to standard logic is really a supplement to it.[39] Even the "relevance" or "implicational" calculi presented as alternative embodiments of a nonstandard entailment conception raise problems of this kind, as (in some cases at least) there seem to be further disagreements about what a theorem of logic is and what *counts* as a system of logic.[40]

These questions—which really raise the issue of the very possibility of genuine deviance from standard logic—are beyond the scope of this book. We note that the issue *has* been raised but must pass on to ask what might prompt a logician to propose a logic he thinks is an alternative to standard logic. For the most part, alternative logics have been proposed based on rejection of the Principle of Bivalence or the Law of Excluded Middle or both. The reasons for wanting to adopt a nonstandard position, however, have varied considerably. We shall merely indicate some of these without seeking to assess them.

(1)

First, some philosophers have held that, in ordinary discourse at least, there are statements that, owing to the vagueness of constituent expressions, are neither true nor false. Consider, for example, the statement that John is in the room. The predicate 'in the room' is sufficiently precise for most situations, but what are we to say if John is standing in the doorway? To some, it has seemed that the statement made in these circumstances is neither true nor false.

Even if one agrees that there are vague predicates in ordinary discourse, it is not clear that an alternative logic is called for. Some philosophers have held that vague sentences simply do not fall within the province of logic.[41] Others, noting that such sentences may very well occur in valid arguments, are willing to accept them as amenable to treatment by logic but feel that no departure from standard logic is called for. Where vague predicates are important in argument, we can seek to make them precise, replacing them with more precise predicates. Much of science has, in fact, proceeded by rephrasing its questions in terms more precise than ordinary language permits, and this road is open as an alternative to adopting a nonstandard logic.[42]

(2)

A second ground for rejecting the Principle of Bivalence (and, some have thought, the Law of Excluded Middle, too), has to do with statements concerning future contingent events. This ground can be reconstructed as an argument:

Consider: (1)   Berger will visit New York on December 1 of next year.

Argument: (2)   (1) is not necessary, nor is it contradictory.

(3)   If (1) is true, then it *has* to come about that Berger will visit New York on December 1 of next year.

(4)   If (1) is false, then it *cannot* come about that Berger will visit New York on December 1 of next year.

(5)   Therefore, (1) is neither true nor false.

Though some philosophers have thought this argument establishes its conclusion and shows the need for an alternative logic,[43] others have thought it is obviously invalid.[44]

It has also been maintained that discoveries in modern physics show the need to reject the Principle of Bivalence and perhaps also the Law of Excluded Middle.[45] In particular, it is widely accepted by physicists as a law of quantum mechanics (the physics of subatomic particles) that it is not possible to ascertain both the position and velocity of a particle. This impossibility is *not* due to the imprecision of instruments of measure; it is not possible for there to *be* such a measurement. It has been argued that this entails that there are some statements that are neither true nor false. More to the point, it has been held that trying to deal with quantum theory using a two-valued logic produces anomalous results, which are avoided by adherence to a nonstandard logic.

An additional challenge to the Law of Excluded Middle has come from a group of logician-mathematicians called *intuitionists*. These mathematicians maintain that mathematical operations are mental operations—i.e., that numbers are mental entities constructed by the mind and the laws of which are laws about the mind's constructions. Thus, a number can be said to exist only if there is a way of constructing it, or counting to it, or "finding" it. Moreover, we can say a number has a certain property only if we can say how to prove the existence of a number with that property. This means that methods are acceptable within mathematics for the intuitionist if, and only if, they are "constructive"— only if they do not presuppose the existence of something of which there is no proof or disproof.[46]

For our purposes, the most important consequence of intuitionism is tied to the requirement of a construction or proof for statements to be assertible. Suppose we have not been able to show that there is a number that has the property F. Nor have we been able to show that there is a number that lacks F. Then, we cannot go on to assert

$$((\exists x)Fx \lor -(\exists x)Fx).$$

Since we do not have a proof of '$(\exists x)Fx$' and we do not have a proof of '$-(\exists x)Fx$', we cannot assume there *is* a proof for one or the other; i.e., since we do not have a proof for either, we would need a proof of the disjunction in order to assert it.

Intuitionism has had a certain attractiveness insofar as it has spawned work in constructivist mathematical technique. In areas dealing with infinite sets it serves as a conservative safeguard against paradoxical results. As a philosophical theory about mathematics and logic, however, it has not won widespread acceptance. Some critics have felt that, in fact, it presupposes standard logic. Some have argued that its epistemological account of the nature of number theory is simply muddleheaded. And the notion of "constructive" method has undergone considerable criticism.[47] But, most importantly, it has been felt that too much of classical mathematics has to be discarded as "non-constructive," and this has seemed too high a price to pay.

(3)

The final sort of nonstandard logic that we shall consider has been given impetus by what some logicians think of as a failure of standard logic to be sufficiently general. Presumably, truths of logic should be true in any possible world, and logic should make no assumptions about the existence of anything. Each of the following, however, is accepted as a truth of logic by standard logicians:

$(\exists x)(Fx \lor -Fx)$

$((x)Fx \supset Fa)$

But the first of these would not be true if there were nothing at all—i.e., if the universe were empty. And the second would not be true if there were nothing that '*a*' denotes. That these are true sentences in standard logic is guaranteed by the standard logician's conception of an interpretation of a symbolism. Since an interpretation always specifies a nonempty domain of objects, it is not possible for the first sentence above to be false in any interpretation. Also, a standard interpretation always assigns an object in the domain to each individual constant. Since each such constant is thus guaranteed a denotation in every interpretation, the second sentence above will be true in every interpretation. But this means that standard logic assumes that something exists (i.e., that the universe is not empty) and that all individual symbols denote.

One sort of response to at least some of these considerations has been the development of logical systems—called *free logics*—that do not make existence assumptions of these kinds. Much contemporary work is being done with free logics and their interpretations, as they appear to have important applications to a number of the difficulties that have spawned nonstandard logics.[48] Underlying these applications is a kind of (nonstandard) interpretation utilized by some proponents of free logic that permits sentences to be neither true nor false. This, in turn, enables a logic interpreted in this way to reflect what some philosophers regard as important relations of "presupposition." A statement, *A*, is said to presuppose a statement, *B*, on the condition that if *B* is false, then *A* is neither true nor false. For example, it has been claimed that

(1)   The present king of France is bald.

presupposes

(2)   There is a person (and only one) who is the present king of France.

in this sense.[49] If (2) is false, then (1) is neither true nor false. Following a proposal by Bertrand Russell, most standard logicians treat (1) as *false* if (2) is false.[50] Expressions such as 'the present husband of Joan', 'the sum of 2 and 3', 'the last boy in the third row' are called *definite descriptions*—they purport to identify a particular thing by a describing phrase. Individual constants and symbolic equivalents of definite descriptions are known as *singular terms*. Free logics are thought by their advocates to present a superior treatment of singular terms than that adopted for most standard logics.

Though nonstandard logics have not been widely adopted (this is part of what makes them nonstandard), much work is being done with them, and it remains to be seen what will emerge insofar as a consensus of logicians' opinions is concerned. One point of great importance, which this survey cannot convey sufficiently, is that the various proposals really call into question much more than particular sentences or inference patterns accepted widely by logicians. In fact, they raise fundamental questions about the nature of logical inference, the nature and use of a logical system, the nature of logical truth, and even what logic is really all about. One particular aspect of such issues concerns the capacity of formal logic to deal with ordinary argumentation. In the next section we shall consider further problems concerning the relation of logic to ordinary discourse and arguments and look at ways of dealing with the difficulties that standard logicians adopt.

6. LOGIC AND ORDINARY LANGUAGE

A number of problems arise for logic when the question of its relationship to ordinary language is posed. These problems can be extremely vexing for the student, since he or she has some concern (usually) for being able to evaluate ordinary arguments that are stated in ordinary language. The devices of logical symbolism have relatively precise uses and meanings that are explicitly specified for them. This is not always true of terms in ordinary discourse. Thus, when we represent ordinary sentences in logical notation, the result sometimes loses something of the meaning of the original or differs from it in some way. The logician, nonetheless, proceeds (usually) as if nothing had gone amiss. To the student this can be alarming. In the first place, he or she can legitimately ask how accurate symbolic translation is of ordinary sentences. And, second, he or she may well ask how it can be justified to test ordinary arguments with symbolic logic if, as is usually conceded, there is a fair measure of variance.

Most logic texts do take the trouble to point out these variances and to offer a justification for the logician's procedure. Nonetheless, it is useful to summarize these in one extended discussion. We shall outline some of the most salient discrepancies between formal logic and ordinary language and then consider what can be said in response.

The initial difficulties arise in propositional logic. The student should recall that propositional logic is a truth-functional logic. This means that the truth or falsity of compound sentences is completely determined by the truth-values of the constituent sentences. From information concerning the truth-values of the constituent sentences it is possible to determine a unique truth-value for the compound. This fact underlies the use of truth-tables, for those tables display the truth-value a compound statement has, given various combinations of the truth-values of the parts. In further discussion we saw that not all sentences that have sentences as parts are truth-functional in this way. For example, sentences of the form: *a* believes that *P*, contain a sentence, but the truth-value of the part does not determine a truth-value for the whole. Such sentences are not truth-functional, and a logical system that deals with their special features (epistemic logic) is intensional. A problem arises, however, when compound sentences in ordinary English are symbolized using the connectives of propositional logic. The difficulty is that there are times when the English compound is *not* strictly truth-functional. This difficulty infects even the connective 'and'. Consider the sentence:

I undressed and I went to bed.

Normally, this would be taken to carry the meaning that the speaker had undressed and gone to bed *in that order*. The 'and' in this sentence is equivalent to 'and then' or 'and subsequently', both of which signify a temporal ordering of the two events. This is completely lost in the truth-functional symbolization. This sentence could be symbolized as:

(P & Q)

The symbolic sentence is true if both components are true, *regardless* of their temporal ordering. Not only would the above English sentence be symbolized in this way by the logician, but so also would sentences employing the English connectives 'yet', 'still', 'but', 'however', 'nevertheless', and several others. At least on some occasions, however, these connectives are employed to convey more than that the two flanking sentences are true. Consider the following use of 'yet':

> Myra experienced much sexist discrimination, yet she was still able to succeed in business.

The sense conveyed here is that a circumstance that has defeated others did not stop Myra. The term 'yet' here functions like 'despite that' or even 'contrary to what might have otherwise been expected'. Such expressions get their force from the (supposed) expectations, understandings, and experiences of speaker and hearer. They are expressive of those background beliefs, attitudes, and so on, and what they express is lost when a sentence such as this is symbolized using a purely truth-functional connective.

By far the most controversial translation problem in propositional logic has to do with the use of '⊃' to symbolize English statements containing 'if __, then __'. A statement having the symbolic form $(A \supset B)$ is taken as logically equivalent to the corresponding symbolic sentence that has the form $-(A \ \& \ -B)$. As logic texts almost universally point out, conditional statements in ordinary discourse almost never assert only what a sentence of the form $-(A \ \& \ -B)$ asserts.

Of course, the logician does not symbolize every English sentence of the form 'If __, then __' as having the symbolic form $(A \supset B)$. Some statements in English having that form are more appropriately rendered with the devices of quantificational logic. Thus, the following would be symbolized in the predicate calculus:

> If anyone enters the King's countinghouse, then that person will be rewarded.

Though the statement above is expressed in the form of an English conditional and though it has some relation to conditionals, its *logical form* is that of a general statement of the kind treated in predicate logic. There are, however, sentences having the 'If __, then __' structure in English that are not readily treated in that way and that appear also not to be truth-functional. Consider the following list:

(1) If Smith presses the button, then the car will start.
(2) If the Dodgers had won the pennant last year, then they would have beaten the Yankees in the World Series.
(3) If Smith or Jones is in the room, and Smith is not, then Jones is in the room.

Statement (1) seems to say more than just that it is not the case that the antecedent is true at the same time the consequent false. It seems to depend for its truth on there being some causal relationship between the antecedent and the consequent. For this reason such conditionals are often called *causal* conditionals.

Statement (2), which is phrased in the subjunctive mood, is often called a *counterfactual* or *contrary-to-fact* conditional. The speaker knows the antecedent to be false, but believes there are appropriate causal laws with which one can tell what events would have taken place had things turned out differently. The truth of the statement is thought to depend on such causal relationships and not merely on the truth-values of the constituent sentences.

The last statement is taken by some logicians as asserting that there is a logical implication between the antecedent and consequent. That relation clearly does not merely assert that it is not the case that the antecedent is true and the consequent false. Such conditionals are sometimes called *implicational* or *logical* conditionals.

The strangeness of symbolizing these sentences using '⊃' is emphasized when we consider the truth-conditions of the material conditional. If we consider (1) and symbolize 'Smith presses the button' with '*P*' and 'the car will start' with '*Q*', the symbolic version of (1) becomes:

(4) $(P \supset Q)$

Suppose we learn that Smith will not press the button. If statement (1) had been a statement made by us, we might still regard (1) as true, or, more likely, we would simply retract or disregard (1) and assert instead:

(5)   If Smith *had* pressed the button, the car *would* have started.

The switch to the *counterfactual* conditional indicates that it is the causal connections between pressing the button and the car's starting to which we are calling attention, not the relationships of truth-values of the component sentences. Suppose, on the other hand, someone else had asserted (1), and we really had doubts that it was an operable car. Would we conclude that what had been asserted was *true* upon learning that Smith would not push the button? Again, our doubt seems to be centered on whether pushing the button could produce the chain of events required to get the car started. Again, our interest (if it is maintained at this point) would likely center on the counterfactual claim (5). But, if (4) is a correct translation of (1), then there should be no need in either case to retreat to (5), since (4) is true if the antecedent is false. If we were in doubt about (1), and (4) represents the truth-conditions of (1), then as soon as we learned the antecedent was false, our doubts should be allayed.

Counterfactual conditionals fare even worse. If counterfactuals are interpreted as material conditions, then they are all true, since they all have false antecedents. But if we have real doubts that the car is in working order, we may continue to question (5) even if we know Smith has not pressed the button.

With respect to implicational conditions, enough has been said in dealing with the implication relation to show that these conditionals are not to be interpreted as material conditionals.

A good part of the problem of the use of '⊃' in symbolizing 'If __, then __' statements is brought out when we consider some rather strange examples. For example:

> (6) If it is raining in New York City, then helium is lighter than hydrogen.

Were someone to assert (6), an initial reaction would probably be puzzlement. Nor would it help if the person attempted to allay our suspicions concerning his or her sanity by saying 'Oh, you see it is *not* raining in New York City'. If (6) is a material conditional, then the falsity of the antecedent makes (6) true. The reason we are puzzled by (6) is that we do not ordinarily take conditionals to be material conditionals. Our expectation is that the speaker is claiming some sort of *connection*—causal or logical—between antecedent and consequent. Of course, there is a connection between the antecedent and consequent of a true material conditional—viz., a connection among their truth-values that rules out that the antecedent is true and the consequent false. But there need be no further connection. So, whereas ordinary conditional statements assert a further connection between antecedent and consequent, material conditionals—the only kind that occur in standard propositional logic—do not assert a further connection.

A similar difficulty has been thought to infect the use of the truth-functional symbol 'V' to symbolize the English 'or'. If 'or' were strictly truth-functional, then from any statement, *A*, that we know to be true, we should be willing to infer (*A* V *B*), where *B* is any statement at all. If we know it is raining in New York City, we should be willing to infer 'either it is raining in New York City or helium is lighter than hydrogen'. People do find such an inference strange, and part of the reason is that we expect there to be *some* kind of connection between the disjuncts in a disjunction. Of course, there is an intimate connection between the material conditional and material disjunction. A sentence of the form (*A* ⊃ *B*) is logically equivalent to one of the form (−*A* V *B*). For such reasons, some philosophers have been led to deny the validity of the principle of inference known in propositional logic as the Principle of Addition:

$$\frac{A}{(A \lor B)}$$

And, of course, they reject the symbolization of ordinary 'or'-statements by means of a purely truth-functional symbol 'V'.

Problems of translation carry over into predicate logic also. These will be summarized very briefly. First, the symbolization of ordinary statements of the form 'All *A* are *B*' has been thought questionable. Symbolized, this becomes '$(x)(Ax \supset Bx)$', which can be read 'For every *x*, if *x* is an *A*, then *x* is a *B*'. Suppose our English sentence is:

(7)   All of Berger's children are blonds.

A paraphrase, as a step toward symbolization, is:

(8)   For every *x*, if *x* is a child of Berger, then *x* is a blond.

There is a subtle but important shift from (7) to (8). (Or at least this is how it seems to many critics of contemporary logic.) Statement (8) introduces the conditional phrase 'if __, then __'. It says that *if* something is a child of Berger's, then it is blond. Moreover, the 'if __, then __' part of the statement is then symbolized using the sign for the material conditional. Thus, if Berger has *no* children, the symbolized sentence is taken as true! But, would we regard someone as having shown (7) is true by pointing out that Berger has no children? Some philosophers believe that statements such as (7) are not taken as true under such circumstances; they think such statements presuppose that there *are* things of the sort spoken of. Some have gone on to contend that where there is failure of reference, the sentences do not express propositions, and others have contended that what is asserted is neither true nor false.

A similar difficulty, as we saw earlier, arises with respect to "singular terms" such as names or definite descriptions—'Bertrand Russell', 'the author of *Mysticism and Logic*'. An example used in many discussions of the problem is:

(9)   The present king of France is bald.

The difficulty is that France has not had a monarchy in quite some time, so there is no present king of France. Is (9) true, or false, or neither? In standard systems of predicate logic, such statements are usually interpreted as implying that the objects referred to exist, so a statement such as (9) is regarded as false. Other philosophers have argued that such sentences as (9) do not assert anything at all, or assert something that is neither true nor false.[51]

There are other difficulties, but these are the main ones that have created philosophical debate and they are the chief sources of students' distrust of modern logic as a device to be applied to ordinary argumentation. Though there is continuing debate among philosophers concerning such matters, the fact is that most, nonetheless, believe symbolic logic to be an acceptable tool. The reasons for this confidence vary somewhat, however.

To begin with, it is often pointed out that many of these difficulties are only apparent. We can illustrate this with respect to the symbolization of 'or' statements. Logicians usually use 'V' to symbolize such sentences unless the possibility of the joint truth of the constituent sentences is explicitly ruled out. Students, however, often argue that 'or' is much more often used in the *exclusive* sense. However, many of the situations in which 'or' seems to be used in an exclusive sense get their force not from the meaning the word 'or' has in such contexts, but because of the situation itself or from the meanings of other words in the sentence. Each of the following illustrates this:

(10)   Either Margaret Court Smith will win the Wimbledon title, or Billie Jean King will win.

(11)   Either Smith will be in New York on Monday at noon, or Smith will be in Los Angeles at 12:30 P.M. on Monday.

In each case we know that if the sentence is true, each disjunct cannot also be true. But, we know this *not* because of the meaning 'or' has, but because we know further information that rules out the joint truth of the disjuncts. Moreover, where this further information is meant to be asserted, and is important for the argument, we have the symbolic devices for bringing it into the argument. That this *is* additional information, however, is made clear by the attempt to render the 'or' in each case as an inclusive, truth-functional 'or'. The explanation of *why* the joint truth is ruled out must appeal to facts having nothing to do with the meaning of 'or'.

Now, some philosophers have held considerations such as these sufficient to show that the English expressions mentioned *really do* have the meanings assigned them by symbolic logic. Consider the various kinds of conditional statement. In each case we had to make reference to background expectations, beliefs, attitudes, and so on, in terms of which we explained them not to be truth-functional. But (so the argument goes), these are not part of the *meaning* of the expression 'if __, then __'. One does not assert the truth of the statements describing the background circumstances that people utilize in understanding what we say.[52] And, of course, if we *do* mean to be asserting these, our symbolism (in most cases) [53] suffices for bringing these explicitly into the argument.

Most logicians, however, do not hold such a view. Most are willing to concede that the symbolic sentences utilized in logic are not always synonymous with the ordinary English statements they symbolize. They think that logic is still useful. For one thing, many logicians are primarily concerned with developing systems to be used in science and mathematics, and the standard logic systems have seemed to them quite adequate for those purposes. Indeed, the fact that logic makes definite truth-value assignments, where ordinary statements might be unclear in this respect, is regarded as an advantage for scientific purposes. As long as we are clear not to take the symbolic expressions to have exactly the meanings of the English counterparts, there is no problem.[54]

Now, philosophers who are primarily concerned with logic as a tool of science and mathematics make a point that virtually all logicians accept. This point is that one should not think of the symbolic sentences as literal "translations" of ordinary English sentences. They usually represent only a part of the meaning of an ordinary English sentence. And the logician is in no position to dictate to anyone how he or she uses his or her language. The logician's concern, when considering arguments in ordinary language, is with abstracting from the sentences their logical form and determining their logical consequences. For this purpose the logician need not be faithful to all of the aspects of the meanings of the words. The ultimate judge of what a person is trying to say is the person himself. The logician does, however, have an apparatus that can unambiguously represent the truth-conditions of statements we make and that can trace out their consequences, given various interpretations. We can then see more clearly the consequences of adopting one or another interpretation. Logic, thus, becomes a tool for clarification and the removal of ambiguity. Indeed, one of its most common philosophical applications is *as* a tool for clarification, rather than as a test for arguments.

If, as most logicians admit, the symbolic representations of ordinary English sentences are not accurate translations of them, how can we be justified in testing ordinary arguments for validity using symbolic logic? In other words, why is this not just a fascinating intellectual game with no direct application to actual argumentation (except, perhaps in mathematics and the best-developed parts of science)?

There is a short answer most logic texts give to this question, which we shall explore at some length. That answer says that in the disputed cases the symbolized sentences capture *part* of the meaning of the English sentences, and, because of this, symbolic logic "works." We need to make more precise the sense in which the symbolic sentences capture part of the meanings of the English and just *why* this means that logic "works."

Our points can be clearly made with respect to conditional sentences. The main source of difficulty with conditionals is that in ordinary discourse they appear to assert a connection of some sort between antecedent and consequent beyond a relationship of truth-values. This means there will be times when the symbolic material conditional used to represent such statements is true, while the ordinary conditional either is false or, as some claim, lacks a truth-value. This is what seems to distinguish ordinary conditionals from material conditionals. There is, however, an important similarity. Each of the ordinary conditionals would be re- garded as false if the antecedent were true and the consequent were false. That is the *one* circumstance when the material conditional is false. So, whenever the material conditional is false, so is the corresponding ordi- nary conditional.[55]

We can put this another way: whenever an ordinary conditional is true, so is its corresponding material conditional. This entails that if we symbolized ordinary conditionals using '$\supset$', the resulting symbolic sen- tence *is implied by* the ordinary conditional. If one looks at the disputed cases where it is argued the ordinary meaning is distorted, it will be noted that in virtually all of them the ordinary sentence implies its symbolic counterpart. Whenever the ordinary sentence is true, so is its symbolic representative. Since there is *some* assignment of truth-values for the parts that determines a truth-value for the whole, these sentences *have a truth- functional aspect*. The significance this fact has for testing arguments can be demonstrated.

Suppose we have an argument expressed in ordinary English, con- sisting of premises, $A_1, A_2, \ldots, A_n$, and a conclusion C. Suppose we symbolize the argument. The result is, in effect, a *new* argument with premises $B_1, B_2, \ldots, B_n$, and conclusion D. We can picture the situa- tion as follows, letting I be the ordinary argument, and letting II be the symbolic argument:

I	II
A_1	B_1
A_2	B_2
.	.
.	.
.	.
A_n	B_n
C	D

Let us suppose there is no problem concerning the symbolization of C, but at least one of the premises of I does raise a difficulty. If the argument in the last paragraph is correct, however, each of $A_1, A_2, \ldots, A_n$ im- plies its corresponding sentence in II. So, whenever $A_1, A_2, \ldots, A_n$ are all true, so are $B_1, B_2, \ldots, B_n$. Suppose we can show that argument II is valid. Then, whenever $B_1, B_2, \ldots, B_n$ are all true, so is D. Thus, whenever A_1, A_2, . . . , A_n are all true, so is D. Since we supposed that D accurately represents the truth-conditions of C, it follows that whenever A_1, A_2, . . . , A_n are all true, so is C. But then argument I is valid.

A similar demonstration cannot be given, however, to show that if argument II is *invalid*, then so is argument I. The reason is that it might be possible for a premise of II to be true when the corresponding premise of I is false. So, while it might be possible for the premises of II all to be true while the conclusion is false, it does not follow that this is true of I. We must take care, then, in cases where the English premises imply the symbolic sentences but the converse does not hold. In such a case a finding of "invalid" may not be reliable.

There is a further proviso to these claims, moreover. We have stipulated that the conclusions of the arguments be equivalent. Where this is not the case, our techniques can again lead us awry. The following is a valid symbolic argument:

$$\frac{P}{(Q \supset P)}$$

But it is not clear that we would regard as valid the following "argument" in ordinary discourse: [56]

It will rain tomorrow.

If the sun is shining tomorrow, it will rain tomorrow.

If the conclusion of this argument were taken as a causal conditional, then we would suppose it to be false (barring *very* unusual circumstances). In any event, we would not take it to be entailed by the statement that it will rain tomorrow. So, our logical techniques can get into difficulties in this sort of case. Now, "arguments" such as this are philosopher's inventions; one rarely (if ever) runs across them in ordinary discourse. Nonetheless, it is important to be aware of such problems, because one use of the devices of symbolic logic is that of discovering the consequences of premises. In that case, we do not already *have* an argument the validity of which is to be tested. We are *constructing* arguments to discover what conclusions are logical consequences of the premises. Since this is done in the symbolism, we must be careful how we render these in English. Once we are aware of the pitfalls, however, this is not a significant problem in practice.

The one remaining problem is that in certain anomalous cases the ordinary English sentence does not even imply the corresponding symbolic sentence. In these cases the symbolism fails and would, again, lead us into error. A rather nice example is given by Professor Howard Pospesel in his book *Propositional Logic:* [57]

> If I will have eternal life if I believe in God, then God must exist. I do not believe in God. Therefore, God exists.

An atheist might be willing to agree to the premises but would deny the conclusion. A test of the argument using truth-functional techniques would show it to be valid; hence, if he agrees to the premises, then he is committed to the conclusion. Now this shows that the initial premise cannot be meant by the atheist as a strictly truth-functional statement. Just what *is* meant makes an interesting problem of analysis.[58]

Cases such as this are *extremely* rare, and when they do occur, the difficulty is usually obvious. In *this* case we know clearly that something has gone wrong as soon as we see the conclusion of the argument. Moreover, the example shows that even in these cases our standard logic has some use, since we have learned something important about the statements that the atheist may be willing to accept.

We can summarize our main conclusions briefly: (1) most of the time the techniques of symbolic logic serve as adequate tests of the validity of ordinary arguments even when the meanings of the ordinary sentences are somewhat misrepresented; (2) there are special kinds of circumstances where these devices fail, but (a) we know what to look for, and (b) even in these cases, the techniques can function as a clarificatory tool, and (c) these cases hardly ever occur in ordinary discourse.

NOTES

1. It is interesting to note a further point. If '*A* implies *B*' is taken as a reading of '($A \supset B$)', and '*A* implies *B*' also means '*B* is deducible from *A*', then we seem to lose important requirements on sets of axioms—viz., that the axioms be consistent with one another and that they be independent of one another. To say they are independent means that none is deducible from the others. To say they are consistent means that all can be true together. If all of these definitions are accepted, however, then if *A* and *B* are independent axioms, ($A \supset -B$) is true and so is ($B \supset -A$). But then it is not possible for *A* and *B* to be true together. Thus, axioms could not be both independent and consistent. This has been pointed out in C. I. Lewis and C. H. Langford, *Symbolic Logic* (New York: Dover, 1932), p. 144.

2. This may be objectionable on the grounds that it encourages "use-mention"

confusions, since 'materially implies' appears to be used to say something *about* statements, while '⊃' is normally employed as a statement connective. Moreover, the additional terminology can confuse students trying to learn the difference between '⊃' and 'logically implies'.

3. See page 11.

4. Such a view clearly takes inference to be a complex *psychological* process with whatever complications for logical theory this would pose.

5. This view is argued for in E. J. Nelson, "Intensional Relations," *Mind*, XXXIX (October, 1930), pp. 440–453.

6. The argument is commonly attributed to Albert of Saxony (1522). See, for example, I. M. Bochenski, *A History of Formal Logic*, 2d ed., trans. and ed. Ivo Thomas (New York: Chelsea Publishing Company, 1970), p. 205.

7. The most widely known of such systems is that of Alan Ross Anderson and Nuel D. Belnap, Jr., "The Pure Calculus of Entailment," *Journal of Symbolic Logic*, XXI (March, 1962), 19–52. The essay is reprinted in a shortened form in Gary Iseminger, ed., *Logic and Philosophy: Selected Readings* (New York: Appleton-Century-Crofts, 1968), pp. 76–108. A discussion of such systems, under the heading of "Implicational Calculi," is in R. Ackermann, *Introduction to Many-Valued Logics*, Monographs in Modern Logic (New York: Dover Publications, Inc., 1967).

8. Lewis and Langford, *Symbolic Logic*, p. 241. Though this book was jointly authored, the chapter on implication was written by Lewis and the views expressed in it are commonly attributed to him.

9. *Ibid.*, p. 248.

10. In a recent article a contemporary logician, John Corcoran, has presented cogent grounds for distinguishing "premise-conclusion" arguments and "demonstrative" arguments. The latter he regards as premises and conclusion together with further statements or "discourse" that is intended to show that the conclusion follows from the premises. See John Corcoran, "Conceptual Structure of Classical Logic," *Philosophy and Phenomenological Research*, XXXIII (1972), 25–47.

11. Chapter II, p. 68.

12. The most influential argument for this position is in Alfred Tarski, *Logic, Semantics, Metamathematics* (Oxford: Clarendon Press, 1956), pp. 408–420. See also Corcoran, "Conceptual Structure of Classical Logic," pp. 41–42.

13. It should not be thought, however, that critics object only to inferences involving logically true or false sentences. The principle of disjunctive syllogism is thought by some to violate a criterion of relevance.

14. Much of the inspiration for these points comes from Richard Cartwright, "Propositions," in *Analytical Philosophy*, ed. R. J. Butler (Oxford: Basil Blackwell, 1962), pp. 81–103.

15. Kant's discussion is in the introductory section of *Critique of Pure Reason*, of which there are numerous extant editions.

16. The discussion that follows draws heavily on W. V. Quine, "Two Dogmas of Empiricism," in *From a Logical Point of View*, 2d ed., rev. (Cambridge, Mass.: Harvard University Press, 1964), pp. 20–46.

17. Gottlob Frege, "On Sense and Reference," in *Translations From the Philosophical Writings of Gottlob Frege*, ed. Peter Geach and Max Black (Oxford: Basil Blackwell, 1960), pp. 56–78.

18. I believe these are the points made by Quine in "Two Dogmas," pp. 29–31.

19. See H. P. Grice and P. F. Strawson, "In Defense of a Dogma," *Philosophical Review,* LXV (1956), pp. 141–158, and Jerrold J. Katz, "Analyticity and Contradiction in Natural Language" in *The Structure of Language: Readings in the Philosophy of Language,* eds. Jerry A. Fodor and Jerrold J. Katz (Englewood Cliffs, N.J.: Prentice-Hall, Inc., 1964), pp. 519–543.

20. See Chapter I.

21. W. V. Quine, *Methods of Logic,* 3d ed. (New York: Holt, Rinehart and Winston, 1972), 1–5; also, W. V. Quine, *Philosophy of Logic,* Foundations of Philosophy Series (Englewood Cliffs, N.J.: Prentice-Hall, Inc., 1970), p. 13.

22. Quine, *Philosophy of Logic,* pp. 1–10.

23. Richard M. Gale, "Propositions, Judgments, Sentences, and Statements," in *The Encyclopedia of Philosophy,* ed. Paul Edwards (New York: The Free Press, 1967), VI, pp. 494–505.

24. See William Kneale and Martha Kneale, *The Development of Logic* (Oxford: The Clarendon Press, 1964), p. 318.

25. Quine, *From a Logical Point of View,* p. 139.

26. Strictly speaking, a *new* sentence is produced with the same truth-value as the original.

27. Quine, *From a Logical Point of View,* p. 140.

28. Of course, the following *is* necessary: If the number of students in Mary's logic class is 30, then the number of students in Mary's logic class is less than 40. What is necessary is a conditional statement. But this does not make either component statement necessarily true.

29. There is an interesting discussion of this in A. N. Prior, *Formal Logic,* 2d ed. (Oxford: The Clarendon Press, 1962), pp. 215–220.

30. See Kneale and Kneale, *The Development of Logic,* p. 605.

31. Quine, *Philosophy of Logic,* p. 34.

32. Rudolf Carnap, *Meaning and Necessity* (Chicago: University of Chicago Press, 1947).

33. For example:

John is the father of Tom.
_____
Tom is not the father of John.

34. The literature can be confusing to students. See, for example, Alan Ross Anderson and Nuel Belnap, Jr., "Entailment," in *Logic and Philosophy,* pp. 76–110. The authors *say* that certain theorems of standard propositional logic that contain '⊃' are false. But they mean that these theorems are false *if* '⊃' is taken as meaning "implies," and if the fact that $(A \supset B)$ is a theorem is taken to permit the deduction of B from A. This means that they do not deny the truth of any standard laws interpreted in the material sense; rather, they object to certain inference patterns.

35. Sometimes these are called *alternative logics.* Standard logic is often called *classical logic.* This is unfortunate terminology, since students may easily confuse "traditional" and "classical" logic. Two books that deal with a variety of nonstandard logics are Nicholas Rescher, *Topics in Philosophical Logic* (Dordrecht, Holland: D. Reidel Publishing Company, 1968), and Susan Haack, *Deviant Logic* (London: Cambridge University Press, 1974). The latter has proved helpful in organizing this section of this book.

36. What we have labeled the *Principle of Bivalence* is sometimes regarded as an

alternative way of stating the law of excluded middle. In recent years, how-ever, it has been held that there is a real difference, as systems have been pro-posed that reject the Principle of Bivalence but still count '$(P \lor -P)$' as a theorem. See Bas C. van Fraassen, "Presuppositions, Supervaluations, and Free Logic," in *The Logical Way of Doing Things*, ed. Karel Lambert (New Haven: Yale University Press, 1969), pp. 67–91.

37. Of course, this follows trivially if one thinks of the two principles as different formulations of the same law.

38. For discussions of these points, see Quine, *Philosophy of Logic*, pp. 80–85; also Haack, *Deviant Logic*, chap. 1.

39. Kneale and Kneale, *The Development of Logic*, pp. 573–574.

40. This point is brought out clearly in Geoffrey Hunter, *Metalogic: An Intro-duction to the Metatheory of Standard First Order Logic* (Berkeley and Los Angeles: University of California Press, 1971), pp. 125–126. Hunter de-parts from the views of Anderson and Belnap with regard to the function of a system used to deduce truths of logic. The disagreement is essentially over the nature of laws and systems of logic.

41. Bertrand Russell, "Vagueness," *Australasian Journal of Philosophy and Psychology*, I (1923).

42. See Haack, *Deviant Logic*, pp. 109–125.

43. Łukasiewicz presented this argument in 1920 along with a three-valued logic.

44. The alleged mistake can be seen as follows. It is pointed out that (3) has the logical form

If *A*, then necessarily *B*.

The sense of this is captured by

Necessarily (if *A*, then *B*).

But, this asserts that the *relation* between the truth-values of *A* and *B* is neces-sary and that does *not* entail

If *A*, then the statement that *B* is a necessary truth.

45. Hans Reichenbach, *Philosophical Foundations of Quantum Mechanics* (Berkeley and Los Angeles: University of California Press, 1944). More re-cently: Karel Lambert, "Logical Truth and Microphysics," in *The Logical Way of Doing Things*, pp. 93–117. Lambert proposed to drop the Principle of Bivalence but adopts a semantics for his system that allows the law of excluded middle as a theorem.

46. A clear account of intuitionism that is useful for students is in Stephen F. Barker, *Philosophy of Mathematics*, Foundations of Philosophy Series (Engle-wood Cliffs, N.J.: Prentice-Hall, Inc., 1964), pp. 72–77.

47. See, for example, Haack, *Deviant Logic*, pp. 99–103.

48. It is pointed out by Bas van Fraassen that such logics have been applied to the difficulties that arise for logic from quantum mechanics, future con-tingent events, certain semantic paradoxes, and other problems. See van Fraassen, "Presuppositions, Supervaluations, and Free Logic," p. 86.

49. A very influential paper in which this claim is argued for is P. F. Strawson, "On Referring," *Mind*, LIX (1950), 320–344. This article is reprinted in

Irving M. Copi and James A. Gould, *Contemporary Readings in Logical Theory* (New York: The Macmillan Company, 1967).

50. Bertrand Russell, "On Denoting," *Mind* XIV (1905), pp. 479–493; reprinted in Copi and Gould, *Contemporary Readings in Logical Theory*, pp. 93–105.

51. Strawson, "On Referring."

52. A suggestion along these lines, applied to conditionals, is found in Quine, *Methods of Logic*, p. 22. An argument like this was outlined to me in private discussion by H. P. Grice; see his paper "Logic and Conversation," in *The Logic of Grammar*, ed. Donald Davidson and Gilbert Harman (Encino and Belmont, Calif.: Dickenson Publishing Company, Inc., 1975), pp. 63–75.

53. Counterfactuals may well be an exception.

54. This seems to be Professor Quine's attitude in his criticisms of Strawson's view. See W. V. Quine, "Mr. Strawson on Logical Theory," *Mind*, LXIII (1953), pp. 433–451.

55. Given any ordinary statement of the form: If A, then B, we can form its *corresponding material conditional* by writing '$(A \supset B)$'. 'If A, then B' is the *corresponding ordinary conditional* of '$(A \supset B)$'.

56. The example is adapted from one invented by Professor Ernest Adams.

57. Howard Pospesel, *Introduction to Logic: Propositional Logic* (Englewood Cliffs, N.J.: Prentice-Hall, Inc., 1974), p. 190. Pospesel attributes an original version of the argument to C. L. Stevenson.

58. An atheist who agreed to the premise would clearly mean:

If, *were* I to believe in God, I would have eternal life, then God exists.

This sentence is a conditional with a counterfactual antecedent. Because the antecedent is counterfactual, this ordinary sentence does not imply its corresponding material conditional. The entire conditional is true if the antecedent is false, and, indeed, the atheist believes the antecedent is false (as well as the consequent). If the antecedent, however, were treated as truth-functional, then since both parts of *it* are regarded as false, the antecedent of the entire conditional would be true and the consequent false, making the entire statement false.

IV

The History of
the Development of Logic

1. INTRODUCTORY COMMENTS

It is not possible to write a comprehensive history of logic that does not presuppose and utilize the various techniques of logic. One must first learn some logic in order to understand and appreciate the important contributions that have been made to the subject. Of course, this is true of the history of any technical subject-matter. Students, however, often are interested in how logic came about and how it has come to its present state. Moreover, the outlines of logic already presented in these materials provide a sufficient basis for us to give a general description of the manner in which logic attained its current state and to indicate some of the main contributors, along with general descriptions of some of their chief contributions. Though we cannot give a true history of the subject, we can outline the general features of its development. This chapter is devoted to such an outline.

In dealing with the history of logic, we must distinguish between the *use* of logic in reasoning and the *study* of logic as a discipline of its own. People reasoned and used logic long before they sought to discover and investigate the principles that underlay their reasoning. It is only the *study* of the principles of sound argumentation that constitutes logic. Many early Greek philosophers, for example, argued about philosophical problems in ways that employ important logical principles. On the other hand, not until Aristotle do we know of any systematic attempt to develop a general theory about the nature of logical consequence or principles of inference. So, in a way, Aristotle is the founder of logic as a discipline, since he wrote a series of works that contain such a theory in

132

an extremely sophisticated, well-developed form. Indeed, in one place [1] Aristotle himself made this very claim—viz., that he was the first to produce such a study.

We may, however, take a somewhat broader view of the matter. The study of the principles and nature of valid argumentation is often furthered by inquiries and investigations that deal, ostensibly, with other matters. For example, in an important philosophical work Plato called attention to the differences between saying something of the form: *A* is *B*, where *A* is said to possess the *property B*, and where *A* is said to be *identical with B*.[2] Modern logicians distinguish the 'is' of predication and the 'is' of identity. As we saw in the very first chapter, inferences involving identity require a very special treatment. Thus, in pointing to errors in philosophical argumentation that were due to confusing these two senses of the Greek equivalent of 'is', Plato was marking a distinction that is relevant to logic. If we include among the contributors to logic those who have conducted inquiries relevant to logic that may have stimulated interest in logical questions, and who suggested avenues of approach to issues within logic, then almost certainly the history of logic began before Aristotle. We shall first outline some of these early influences on the course of logic prior to Aristotle.

2. THE EARLIEST INFLUENCES

The earliest studies that are relevant to logic, of which we have knowledge, were made in the areas of geometry and early Greek philosophy. The Pythagoreans, a circle of philosophers who lived in the sixth and fifth centuries B.C., made important discoveries in mathematics and geometry, and, by the third century B.C., Euclid wrote his famous *Elements,* which was the first known presentation of geometry as a subject-matter developed from a base of axioms. Thus, the early Greeks founded, in geometry, the axiomatic method—the presentation and arrangement of a body of knowledge as a set of deductions from initial assumptions, utilizing terms defined on the basis of a small set of primitive terms. This constituted the presentation of geometry as a *deductive system.* Geometrical truths were *deduced* on the basis of a set of axioms.

Also, as philosophical discussion developed, various techniques of argumentation and refutation came to be employed that have played important roles in logic when codified as principles. An early Greek philosopher named Parmenides held the view that reality is one—i.e., is eternal, indivisible, immovable, and unchanging. On this view, all change and motion would be merely illusory. This theory was defended in the fifth century B.C. by Zeno, a philosopher of Elea (a Greek colony), who attempted to show that any alternative theory led to impossible results and must therefore be rejected. A brief example of such arguments will suffice. Suppose an arrow is in motion. At any particular moment it occupies a particular space. If it occupies a space, it is at rest in that place. Since at every moment of its "flight" it is at rest, it is always at rest; therefore, it is never in motion. Such a method of refutation is known as *reductio ad impossible*. We are led to reject a statement or theory because from it we can deduce results that are contradictory; thus, the theory "reduces" to an impossibility. Similarly, Socrates, the teacher of Plato, often refuted opponents by showing their views yielded false or "absurd" results. The form of such a refutation is as follows: Let the opponent's statement be *P*. We show that *P* implies *Q*. But *Q* is false, or absurd, and so must be rejected. But, if not *Q* is true, then *P* cannot be true. So, we must reject *P*. Such an argument corresponds to the logical principle known as *Modus Tollens*.

Another philosopher who conducted studies of interest to logicians is Plato, who pursued problems in the philosophy of language that are relevant to issues in logic. Among the most important of these, of course, was his showing the distinction between the sense 'is' has when a predication is made and when an identity is asserted.

Finally, among early influences on the development of logic, we must mention the early study of various logical paradoxes and puzzles. As these, however, were pursued by a group of philosophers who made other important contributions to logical theory itself, we shall defer our discussion of these puzzles until after our treatment of Aristotle.

3. ARISTOTLE AND THE DEVELOPMENT OF SYLLOGISTIC LOGIC

Some commentators on the history of logic regard Aristotle as the founder of logic. As indicated earlier, there is an important sense in which this is surely correct. His was the first attempt we know of to treat logic and its techniques as a special subject-matter in which a theory is developed and a method of logic organized. Had Aristotle merely been the first to do this, his achievement would be noteworthy. The fact is that the theory he developed was itself one of the most important contributions ever made to logic—a theory which, for the most part, dominated logic until the present century. Though logic has never exclusively studied the theory of the syllogism and there have been periods when either it was regarded as unimportant or other studies predominated, syllogistic logic has been a Greek legacy that has largely dominated logic texts. Such an achievement by a single man is, indeed, remarkable.

Aristotle's work in logic is contained in a series of books that, as a body, are known as the *Organon*. The topics actually discussed range over metaphysics, philosophy of language, modal logic, and the theory of the syllogism. The latter, of course, is of greatest interest to us.

In Chapter I we gave a very brief characterization of syllogisms. The outline presented, however, corresponds more closely to the way the theory has come down to us from later logicians than it does to Aristotle's presentation. Let us note some of the features of Aristotle's theory of the syllogism.

Aristotle's theory makes use of three sets of doctrines: (a) an analysis of the logical constituents of propositions, (b) his theory of opposition, (c) his theory of conversion. We shall briefly explain these. Every sentence that may occur in a syllogism has both a subject term and a predicate term. If one asserts 'some man is white', the term 'man' is the subject term and 'white' is the predicate term. Moreover, every statement in a syllogism is either affirmative or negative, according to whether the statement asserts or denies that the predicate "belongs to" the subject. Finally, every statement that is either a premise or conclusion of a syllogism is either universal or particular.[3] A universal statement asserts or denies something of all things of a certain kind—e.g., 'every man is white', 'no man is white'. A particular statement asserts or denies something of some things of a certain kind—e.g., 'some man is white', 'some man is not white'. Since the Middle Ages these four forms of statement have been designated by the vowels **A**, **E**, **I**, and **O**. **A** statements are universal affirmative, **E** statements are universal negative, **I** statements are particular affirmative, and **O** statements are particular negative.

Aristotle was interested in the logical relations among statements of these forms, and his theories of opposition and conversion express important logical relationships among them. The theory of opposition concerns sentences having the same subject and predicate terms. According to this theory, the **A** and **O** sentences and the **E** and **I** sentences are *contradictories,* since, of each pair, it is necessarily the case that one is true and the other false. The **A** and **E** sentences are not contradictory, since it *is* possible for both to be false; however, since it is *not* possible for both to be true—i.e., *if* one is true, the other is false—they are called *contraries.* In later times these relationships came to be summarized in a diagram known as the *Square of Opposition* found in virtually all texts in traditional logic. This diagram also picks out further relationships that Aristotle failed to explicitly mention when giving this theory of opposition.

Aristotle's theory of conversion asserts important entailment relations among propositions. The laws of conversion were stated in several forms and examples given. One very significant presentation by Aristotle was as follows:

If *A* belongs to no *B*, then *B* will not belong to any *A*.
If *A* belongs to all *B*, then *B* will belong to some *A*.
If *A* belongs to some *B*, then *B* will belong to some *A*.

These are meant as statements of logical implication and permit the inference of one proposition of a certain form from another of which it is a logical consequence. The laws of conversion were employed by Aristotle in this fashion.

We should note in passing a certain problem that the theory of opposition and theory of conversion pose. If one accepts all of the laws of opposition and conversion, then, from a statement of the form 'No *A* is *B*', we can deduce 'No *B* is an *A*' (by conversion), and from that we can conclude 'Some *B* is not an *A*' (according to the theory of opposition). Now, this is perfectly in order, *if* we assume that there *are* *A*'s and there *are* *B*'s—i.e., if we assume there are some things that are *A*'s and there are some things that are *B*'s. But if we pick for our *A*'s or *B*'s terms that do not in fact apply to existing things—e.g., "round squares"—we get into trouble. Consider the statement 'No material object is a round square'. According to the theory, we can convert this to 'No round square is a material object'. And this is taken to imply 'Some round square is not a material object'. This last statement is normally taken to imply that there *is* a round square that is not a material object! Thus, Aristotle's theory is a theory about certain forms of statement that contain terms assumed to apply to existing things.

Traditional logic differs from modern logic on this point. Traditional logic permits the inference of 'Some *A* are *B*' from 'All *A* are *B*'. Modern logic does not permit the inference, since it is held that *if* there are no *A*'s, then the latter is true, while the former is false. The traditional view, which presupposes that all the terms apply to existents, is often referred to as *the doctine of existential import*. Of course, if the modern logician makes the same assumptions as the traditional logician, his logical theory will be identical. Since that is the case, we need not suppose there is a disagreement; we can say that traditional logic is somewhat more limited in that it is part of the logic of general terms that refer to existing things.

We cannot here present Aristotle's theory of the syllogism in detail, nor is it the function of this chapter to do so. We need only note its most important features. Every syllogism has three sentences—two premises and a conclusion—and each sentence is of one of the four forms indicated. Aristotle stated the forms of valid syllogisms most often by means of conditional statements. For example, the syllogistic figure known later as *Barbara* would be described by Aristotle as: if *A* is predicated of all *B* and *B* of all *C*, it is necessary for *A* to be predicated of all *C*. In effect, what this tells us is that any syllogism that has premises of the form 'All *B* is *A*', and 'All *C* is *B*' and a conclusion of the form 'All *C* is *A*' is valid. The core of Aristotle's theory of the syllogism was his listing of the valid combinations of premises and conclusions—i.e., his systematic study of the valid forms of syllogisms. Moreover, of great interest were his methods of determining *that* a given combination of premises and conclusions is valid or not.

Aristotle began his exposition by separating out what he called *perfect* from *imperfect* syllogisms. The perfect syllogisms (e.g., Barbara, given above) are such that the necessary connection between premises and conclusion is "evident" with no further information. He listed four of these. Two of the four came to play a special role, as we shall see. The other possible combinations of the four forms of propositions for premises and conclusions were accepted or rejected by some manner of demonstration, rather than by appeal to the intuitive self-evidence of the validity or invalidity of the argument-form. These methods are important. First, *some* of the possible combinations were rejected on the basis of *counter-examples*—i.e., by citing examples of arguments that have the forms under consideration such that the premises are true and the conclusion is false. No argument-form can be valid if it is possible for an argument with that form to be invalid. Second, Aristotle showed that *some* of the possible combinations *do* make valid syllogisms by showing that they can be "reduced" to the first two "perfect" syllogisms. This is done by using the laws of conversion and opposition. If, when those laws are applied to the premises and/or conclusion of an argument, the result is a "perfect" syllogism, the original argument is valid. Finally, Aristotle used a method known as *reductio ad impossible*. This method involved taking a *denial* of the conclusion along with one of the original premises and constructing a new, valid syllogism with a conclusion that contradicts the other premise in the original argument. Such a process shows that anyone who asserts the original premises, but denies the conclusion, is involved in a contradiction; thus, there is a necessary connection between the premises and conclusion.

Of very great interest was Aristotle's showing that *all* the valid syllogisms he isolated could be "reduced to" the perfect syllogisms. In effect, he had shown that the first two syllogisms could be formulated as axioms from which all the others (formulated as conditionals) could be deduced!

Aristotle's achievement is truly amazing. With virtually no background work to rely on he (1) invented the use of variables to express logical laws in their most general form, (2) gave the first systematic (and nearly complete) theory of the syllogism, (3) made important contributions to that portion of the philosophy of language that bears on logical theory, (4) systematically employed the method of "counterexamples" to show the invalidity of argument-forms, (5) presented the seeds of an axiomatic development of a logical theory. In addition, he made contributions to modal logic that we cannot survey here.

4. OTHER ANCIENT CONTRIBUTIONS

Aristotle's work was continued by his students, one of whom, Theophrastus, is usually credited with important additions to the theory—a further set of valid syllogisms. Moreover, he is thought to have developed a theory of "hypothetical" syllogisms—i.e., ones in which all sentences have the form 'if __, then __.' Had this theory been well developed, it would be of significance, since such a theory is clearly a part of propositional logic—an area left virtually untreated by Aristotle. Such appears not to be the case, however.

About the same time Aristotle began his work, a group of logicians known as the Megarians were conducting important studies that came later to influence another group of philosophers known as the Stoics. Thus, for a period of almost two hundred years, non-Aristotelian logic was pursued. Unfortunately, little of this work survives. These philosophers investigated four areas: (1) they invented a number of logical "paradoxes" that provide a challenge to logical theory (e.g., a man says that he is lying; is what he says true or false?); (2) they made important studies of modal logic; (3) they investigated at length the nature of conditional propositions and, in the process, developed many of the modern theories of the nature of logical implication; (4) they made the first extensive studies of propositional logic and worked out many of its basic laws.[4]

For a very long time, little original work was done beyond the Aristotelian and Stoic accomplishments. Aristotle and Chrysippus, who was the most important and influential Stoic, were the leading figures of ancient logic. Until the first half of the twelfth century most work in logic consisted of translations and commentaries on the logic of these two schools. Boethius, the most noteworthy logician of this period (he was born around A.D. 470–80), is most important for his Latin translations and commentaries on Aristotle, which provided the chief information on the ancients until the twelfth century. He also invented the "square of opposition" and set forth much of the terminology employed in traditional logic. Beyond this, there is little to report concerning the development of logic until the twelfth century, at which time a brief period (about 200 years) of fruitful investigation was initiated.

5. MEDIEVAL LOGIC

Though medieval logic appears to have been extremely sophisticated and original, we shall not outline its contributions at length—for two reasons. First, this contribution has only recently come to be studied closely, and many of the medieval writings still have not been translated. Second, a large part of the medieval contribution consists of studies in the philosophy of language and in modal logic, which we have chosen not to pursue. In fact, there are four areas in which the medievals worked: (1) they developed an analysis of the properties of terms, which led them to the important distinction between *using* a term (to talk about what the term refers to) and *mentioning* or talking about a term; (2) they devoted a great deal of time and made acute observations about logical puzzles, such as the Liar's Paradox; (3) they developed a logic of modalities; and (4) they worked out a theory of sound *consequentiae* that was, in large measure, a theory of the sentential calculus.

Of course, there was no *one* theory for this period, but a set of common subjects to which various thinkers contributed. It is thus impossible to outline *the* theory of *consequentiae*. Some writers took a *consequentia* to be a conditional statement; others took it to be an argument in which premises and conclusion are connected by 'therefore', thus indicating a logical relationship. The same writer sometimes would employ both uses, and those who employed the latter still referred sometimes to the "antecedent" and "consequent," meaning thereby the premises and conclusion of an argument. Moreover, the theory of *consequentiae* sometimes was regarded as the whole of deductive logic, including among *consequentiae* valid syllogisms and the laws of conversion. Others thought of it as a theory that supplemented Aristotelian logic. What is most distinctive about it is that it picked out important laws of sentential logic (apparently without its authors' having much acquaintance with Stoic logic). The study of *consequentiae* led also to important investigations of the truth-conditions of conditional statements and of the nature of logical consequence.

Before leaving off our discussion of the medievals, we might note that they made a distinction between *categorematic* and *syncategorematic* terms that parallels the modern distinction between non-logical terms and logical constants. Moreover, they investigated the truth-conditions of sentences containing the logical constants.

In the mid-1400's began what, to modern observers, appears to have been a 400-year decline in the quality of logical work. A period of anti-Aristotelianism set in, supplanted by a concern with rhetoric and style that, though having a place among human concerns, is not especially conducive to the development of rigorous logic. The best-known writer of the sixteenth century was Peter Ramus, who attacked Aristotle in a number of ways, though what little seems of value in his own work is, for the most part, Aristotelian in derivation. The sixteenth and seventeenth centuries saw a number of logic manuals published, but formal studies were not popular in a period concerned with style and elegance, and the logic texts tended toward incompetence. In the later part of the seventeenth century the most influential logic text was a book often referred to as the *Port Royal Logic* (its title was *La logique ou l'art de penser*), which tended to view logic as closely allied with the theory of knowledge and with psychology. The *Port Royal Logic* helped influence the view of the nature of logic that we labeled *psychologism* in Chapter I. Its only notable direct contribution to logical theory is a distinction that became widely adopted between the *comprehension* of a general term— the set of attributes without which the concept would be destroyed—and the *extension* of a general term—the set of things to which the term applies.

One final contribution of this period should be mentioned. This is the doctrine of the distribution of terms. A term is said to be distributed in a statement if the statement attributes a property to everything to which the term applies. Thus, the term 'men' is distributed in 'All men have a heart' but is undistributed in 'Some men have a heart'. The significance of this bit of analysis is that it enables the logician to set up mechanical rules for testing syllogisms for validity, according to whether or not certain terms are distributed in the sentences in the argument.[5]

With the German philosopher Gottfried Wilhelm Leibniz being the primary (but not only) exception, it was not until the eighteenth century that important developments worthy of note took place. That period marks the beginning of modern logic, and Leibniz was its precursor.

6. MODERN LOGIC

The past hundred or so years have seen a tremendous advance in the development of logic. So many figures have been involved that it is not possible to present in short compass a detailed history of modern logic. Moreover, the innovations introduced very quickly require a degree of expertise that we have sought not to presuppose. What we can do is to describe the most crucial high points of this development to give the student a picture of how logic came to its present state.

To begin with we must mention Leibniz, who more or less set out a conception of what logic should aspire to, which contemporary developments mirror to a certain extent. Leibniz's plan was to develop a universal language for science, ideally suited to it so as to reflect in the form of statements the nature of reality. Leibniz thought all scientific ideas could be reduced to a relatively few "simple," unanalyzable ideas in terms of which all others could be defined. New discoveries would become possible by the breaking down and putting together of ideas, much in the same way that calculation in mathematics proceeds. Thus, he conceived of scientific knowledge as mathematized and of investigation as proceeding through calculation. The concepts of a special language for logic, and of discovery through calculation, have run throughout the history of modern logic, so that, while few today would endorse Leibniz's view concerning all of a science of reality, no one denies the importance for logic of this conception of that discipline.

One of the most important steps taken toward this ideal for logic was the contribution of the English mathematician, George Boole, who lived from 1815 to 1864. About the middle of the nineteenth century Boole developed a kind of abstract algebra, the operations of which ("addition," "multiplication," and so on) he thought of as necessarily involved in all thinking. This he believed because the symbolization he presented could be interpreted in a way that results in a logic of classes, so that it could be used to represent the various **A, E, I,** and **O** forms of statement and logical relations among them. Boole had set out a system of symbols and laws for combinations among them. He showed that if certain of the symbols are taken to represent ("elect") classes and others to represent possible ways of combining, or taking apart, or relating classes, then the laws of combining the symbols become laws concerning classes. He then showed that the symbols could *also* be interpreted in a manner permitting the representation of the statement-forms of traditional logic! Boole did not stop here, however; he went on to show that with the addition of one further law, there is an interpretation of the algebra that yields the theory of propositional logic *and* the ordinary algebra of the numbers 0 and 1. Boole had mathematized much of logic, thus realizing in part Leibniz's ideal, and had worked out the basic elements of the concept of an uninterpreted system that can express the logical structure of otherwise diverse theories.

Much improvement was made on Boole's system by others. We should note the important contributions of Augustus De Morgan (1806–1871) and Charles Sanders Peirce (1839–1914), the American philosopher, to the development of an algebra of relations—a branch of logic in which traditional logic was virtually wholly deficient. We must skip over further developments along these lines in order to talk of the most important contributor to modern logic, Gottlob Frege (1848–1925).

All commentators agree that Frege was to modern logic what Aristotle was to traditional logic. Unfortunately, we can only briefly summarize his achievement here. It was Frege's view that arithmetic can be "reduced" to logic—i.e., that all arithmetical statements can be restated using only concepts of logic, and that all arithmetical truths can be deduced from the laws of logic (though not from what we called in Chapter I "basic logic"). To show this, Frege first set out the criteria for a language of logic and for a system of logic. All terms are to be defined by a set of basic primitives; criteria for all meaningful sentences are indicated at the outset; and all permissible inference rules are set out in the beginning. Thus, he set out precise criteria for an axiom system. He constructed such a system for the sentential calculus and thus was the first to present a fully axiomatized, consistent, and complete system of the sentential calculus. He invented the modern method of *quantifiers* that "range over" variables. Instead of writing 'All A are B', we use a symbolism that translates, roughly, as 'For every x, if x is an A, then x is a B'. This may seem a small change, but it has tremendous advantages. For one thing, it provides a suitable manner of symbolizing relational propositions and thus facilitates the statement of the logic of relations. Frege then added axioms and inference rules governing sentences containing the quantifiers to his system, which then was sufficient for all of first-order predicate logic. With this achievement he had presented a unified, general theory of logic that included all of modern, first-order quantification theory. The system could also incorporate all of traditional logic, and it encompassed all of propositional logic. He then invented second-order logic and showed how arithmetic and other parts of mathematics could be "reduced" to this logic.

Though Frege's chief works presenting his logic were published in 1879 and 1884, his work was not well known until Bertrand Russell called attention to it in his book *The Principles of Mathematics* (1903). Russell shared Frege's view on the reducibility of arithmetic and other parts of mathematics to logic, and he had discovered that the class theory employed by Frege in his later work yields a contradiction (Russell's Paradox, outlined in Chapter I). He attempted with Alfred North Whitehead to develop Frege's program further and also repaired Frege's set theory so as not to produce the contradiction. This was done in a monumental work called *Principia Mathematica,* published in three volumes between 1910 and 1913.

With this basic outline of the development of modern logic until the first part of the present century, we can go on to describe further important contributions that help fill in that outline.

First, it must be pointed out that the traditional, Aristotelian logic had not been abandoned by logicians. One development of traditional logic was the invention of systems of diagrams or circles for representing categorical statements and for testing syllogisms for validity. Such a set of diagrams was published by the mathematician Leonhard Euler in 1768. The most widely used diagrams today, however, were the invention of an English logician, John Venn, in his book of 1881, *Symbolic Logic*. The circles in the diagrams represent classes, and with the circles it is possible to represent the class relationships asserted in categorical statements. Most texts even today present some version of these diagrams. Their prime utility consists in their use as a test for the validity of syllogistic and other arguments.[6] Venn was very much influenced by George Boole and developed the diagrams in connection with Boole's algebra.

An interesting aspect of the progress of modern logic is that various discoveries of importance either went unnoticed, or were misunderstood, or were rejected by the principal logicians or mathematicians who were working in logic. We have already mentioned that Frege's work, some of it published as early as 1879, was largely ignored until brought to general recognition by Bertrand Russell in 1903. Another striking example is the work of Charles Sanders Peirce. Though Peirce was not without influence—we have already mentioned his contribution to the development of the logic of relations—he made a number of discoveries and contributions that anticipated similar work of later writers, or that were more influential through the work of others. For example, entirely independently of Frege, he invented a notation for the universal and existential quantifiers,[7] and he produced a complete set of axioms for propositional logic, as had Frege. In addition, he showed that it was possible to express all truth-functional connectives using only one (meaning 'neither ___, nor ___'). Though Peirce made this discovery in 1880, it had to be rediscovered in 1913 by H. M Sheffer. Also in 1880 Peirce devised a truth-table method for displaying the truth-conditions of compound statements. The contemporary use of truth-tables in a systematic way and as a test procedure in propositional logic dates to the work of Ludwig Wittgenstein and Emil Post in 1920.

A further development we must mention in connection with this history is that of the mathematical theory of sets or classes. Set theory was largely invented by Georg Cantor during the last quarter of the nineteenth century. A set, in his view, is just any "collection" of objects of thought or perception. The set is said to *contain* its objects; the objects are *members* of the set. If all members of a set ϕ are members also of a set ψ, then ϕ is a subset of ψ. The set of natural numbers (0, 1, 2, . . .) is an infinitely large set. It has a special peculiarity—the set of odd numbers is a subset of the set of natural numbers, and it, too, is infinitely large. Moreover, it is an easy matter to put each natural number in a one-one correspondence with an odd number. Thus, we can say that the set of natural numbers is the same "size" as one of its subsets. Cantor then showed that there are infinite sets that cannot be put in one-one correspondence with the natural numbers—e.g., the real numbers between 0 and 1. This showed that there is a set that outruns the natural numbers and that is thus larger (in some sense) than the set of natural numbers.

Using his theory of sets, Cantor was able to give exact definitions to such mathematical concepts as infinity and cardinal and ordinal number. His work was clearly a forerunner to Frege's development of arithmetic. The sort of set theory that emerged, however, was shown by Russell to lead to contradictions, and a variety of set theories have been devised that attempt to avoid these results.[8]

The various contemporary set theories are presented in axiomatic form. Axiomatization is an important tool for achieving clarity, precision, and economy of rules and assumptions. The standard method of presenting logic from the time of Frege's work until 1934 was in the form of an axiom system. In 1934 Stanislaw Jaskowski and Gerhard Gentzen (working independently) developed systems of natural deduction, and it is these that are most often taught in contemporary logic texts. The systems used are usually variants of Gentzen's.

It remains only to mention the current work being done in logic. In the first place, this century has seen metalogic become a major concern of logicians, and some of the most impressive results in the history of logic have been obtained. Two of these have been mentioned earlier in this book, and they bear repetition here.

Of all the great advances made in modern logic, two of the most important are proofs of certain limits of known methods of logic. Two ideals that modern logicians had set for themselves were to be able to "calculate" all logical truths by means of a system of logic and to be able to "reduce" all of mathematics to logic. In the early 1930's Kurt Gödel proved that any system of second-order logic, or set theory that is sufficient for expressing arithmetic, is such that if it is consistent, then it is incomplete.[9] Thus, no system of logic can capture all of mathematics. In 1935 Alonzo Church showed that, given certain assumptions that most logicians accept (known as *Church's Thesis*), there can be no decision procedure for first-order predicate logic (this is known as *Church's Theorem*). What this shows, of course, is that not even all of basic logic can be reduced to "caculation," independent of the application of human ingenuity.

We can list other noteworthy contributions to logic in the present century. Prior to his "incompleteness" proof of higher-order logic, Gödel had proved (in 1930) that first-order logic *is* complete. This is somewhat remarkable in light of Church's proof that no decision-procedure can be given for first-order logic. Other work of significance includes the development of formal semantics, largely spurred by the work of Alfred Tarski (a Polish logician who came to Berkeley). Tarski gave a precise (and widely accepted) definition of truth for formal languages (1933) and defined other semantic concepts (e.g., logical consequence) in a rigorous way. He also helped to establish metalogic and metamathematics as precise studies. Modal logic was given impetus by the work of C. I. Lewis, who propounded five modal systems in 1932. Other important work in modal logic was done by Rudolf Carnap (1947) and G. H. von Wright (1951). Saul Kripke gave an important completeness proof in modal logic in 1959.

Finally, we should mention the contributions of Willard Van Orman Quine. Much work in intensional logic has been in response to Quine's critical attacks (see Chapter III), and it is fair to say that serious contemporary work in the philosophy of logic must at least take account of his views. He has also made important contributions to set theory and mathematical logic. One of his chief concerns has been the relation between language and the world, and he has proposed and defended a criterion by which to decide what kinds of objects a given discourse is committed to presupposing as existing (his criterion of "ontological commitment").

Contemporary logicians are busy pursuing issues in the philosophy of logic (such as those described in Chapter III), the development of nonstandard logics, and the application of logical systems and techniques to problems of philosophy, mathematics, linguistics, and social science. Much of this work involves fundamental questions in logic, and the refined tools of modern logic permit more exact discussion of the problems. It is fair to say that this is a period of very great activity that could have far-reaching results in both the theory and the application of logic.

NOTES

1. Aristotle, *De Soph. Elenchus* 34 (184ᵃ8).
2. The distinction underlies Plato's discussion in the *Sophist* 251–259.
3. Actually, Aristotle also took note of *singular* and *indefinite* propositions, but, as these do not figure in his presentation of the syllogistic, they are not treated here.
4. The outline given here of ancient logic is widely accepted. Recent work, however, has called into question various aspects of the account. These are matters beyond this book. For further discussion see John Corcoran, "Aristotle's Natural Deduction System," in *Ancient Logic and Its Modern Interpretations,* ed. John Corcoran (Dordrecht, Holland: D. Reidel Publishing Company, 1974), pp. 85–131; and Michael Frede, "Stoic vs. Aristotelian Syllogistic," *Archiv für Geschichte der Philosophie,* Vol. LVI (1974), pp. 1–32.
5. An accessible presentation is in Wesley Salmon, *Logic,* 2d ed., Foundations of

Philosophy Series (Englewood Cliffs, N.J.: Prentice-Hall, Inc., 1973), pp. 51–56.

6. A somewhat different set of diagrams was invented by Lewis Carroll. See Lewis Carroll, *Symbolic Logic and Game of Logic* (New York: Dover Publications, Inc., and Berkeley Enterprises, 1958). Students interested in logic diagrams should see Martin Gardner, *Logic Machines and Diagrams* (New York: McGraw-Hill Book Company, 1958).

7. Peirce based his symbolism on that of a student, O. H. Mitchell. Peirce used 'Π' as the universal quantifier and 'Σ' as the existential quantifier.

8. A brief survey is found in W. V. Quine, *Methods of Logic,* 3d ed. (New York: Holt, Rinehart and Winston, Inc., 1972), chap. 46, and, more fully, in W. V. Quine, *Set Theory and Its Logic,* rev. ed. (Cambridge, Mass.: Harvard University Press, 1963 and 1969).

9. Readable summaries of the essentials of Gödel's proof are found in Quine, *Methods of Logic,* pp. 183–185, and Stephen F. Barker, *Philosophy of Mathematics,* Foundations of Philosophy Series (Englewood Cliffs, N.J.: Prentice-Hall, Inc., 1964), pp. 94–97. A more detailed presentation is that of Ernest Nagel and James R. Newman, *Gödel's Proof* (New York: New York University Press, 1958).

A Selected Bibliography

LOGIC TEXTS

BARKER, STEPHEN F. *The Elements of Logic* (2d ed.). New York: Mc-Graw-Hill Book Company, 1974. A beginner's text, which covers traditional and modern deductive logic, fallacies, and inductive reasoning.

COPI, IRVING M. *Introduction to Logic* (4th ed.). New York: The Macmillan Company, 1972. Widely used introductory book, which covers language and logic, syllogistic and symbolic logic, and induction.

KAHANE, HOWARD. *Logic and Philosophy: A Modern Introduction* (2d ed.). Belmont, Calif.: Wadsworth Publishing Company, Inc., 1973. Somewhat more advanced treatment of the same topics as the previous texts. Also, chapters on logic and philosophy: paradoxes, analyticity, modal, epistemic, deontic logic, elementary set theory.

KAMINSKY, JACK, and ALICE KAMINSKY. *Logic: A Philosophical Introduction*. Reading, Mass.: Addison-Wesley Publishing Company, 1974. Some discussion of fallacies, language, and induction, but concentrates on modern deductive logic. Very helpful discussions of philosophical issues along the way.

LAMBERT, KAREL, and BAS C. VAN FRAASSEN. *Derivation and Counterexample: An Introduction to Philosophical Logic*. Encino and Belmont, Calif.: Dickenson Publishing Company, Inc., 1972. A sophisticated, somewhat advanced text in symbolic logic. Presents semantic tableaux, logic of singular terms, and some metalogic. Outlines and defends system of free logic.

MATES, BENSON. *Elementary Logic* (2d ed.). New York: Oxford University Press, 1972. A model of precision in a beginning text. Presents clear and precise notion of an interpretation and important semantical concepts of logic. Discussion of axiomatic theories. Excellent outline of the history of logic.

NEIDORF, ROBERT. *Deductive Forms: An Elementary Logic.* New York: Harper & Row, Publishers, 1967. A good beginner's text. Presents rules of logic as based on intuitively obvious modes of ordinary reasoning, thus developing technical skills from capacities the reader already possesses.

POSPESEL, HOWARD. *Predicate Logic: Introduction to Logic.* Englewood Cliffs, N.J.: Prentice-Hall, Inc., 1976. A sequel to the author's earlier book on propositional logic. Together, they make a good introduction to basic logic. Clear and readable. Restrictions on quantifier rules are simplified, diagram techniques are covered, and disproofs by interpretations are used.

POSPESEL, HOWARD. *Propositional Logic: Introduction to Logic.* Englewood Cliffs, N.J.: Prentice-Hall, Inc., 1974. A clear, very readable introduction to the elementary portion of modern logic. Utilizes examples from everyday affairs, making it of greater interest to students.

PURTILL, RICHARD L. *Logic for Philosophers.* New York: Harper & Row, Publishers, 1971. Very comprehensive account of elementary and advanced logic, including modal, epistemic, and deontic logic. Some discussion of ordinary language, probability, and scientific inference. Philosophical discussion throughout.

QUINE, W. V. *Methods of Logic* (3d ed.). New York: Holt, Rinehart and Winston, Inc., 1972. Highly original, sophisticated introductory text by one of today's leading logicians. Though concentrating on technique, contains a bonanza of historical and philosophical material. Last chapter is an excellent outline of more advanced matters.

PHILOSOPHY OF LOGIC

COPI, IRVING M., and JAMES A. GOULD, eds. *Readings on Logic* (2d ed.). New York: The Macmillan Company, 1972. Contains historical and contemporary selections on issues in the philosophy of logic, with an emphasis on historically important matters. For beginners.

COPI, IRVING M., and JAMES A. GOULD, eds. *Contemporary Readings in Logical Theory.* New York: The Macmillan Company, 1967. More advanced readings on contemporary issues, including modal, deontic, and many-valued logics.

ISEMINGER, GARY, ed. *Logic and Philosophy: Selected Readings.* New York: Appleton-Century-Crofts, 1968. Primarily contemporary readings on philosophical issues. Good for beginners.

QUINE, W. V. *Philosophy of Logic.* Foundations of Philosophy Series. Englewood Cliffs, N.J.: Prentice-Hall, Inc., 1970. Most suited for advanced students. Outlines Quine's views on a wide range of issues in a succinct form.

METALOGIC, MATHEMATICS AND LOGIC

BARKER, STEPHEN F. *Philosophy of Mathematics.* Foundations of Philosophy Series. Englewood Cliffs, N.J.: Prentice-Hall, Inc., 1964. A very clear presentation of the most important topics in the philosophy of mathematics. Highly recommended for students interested in this subject.

DE LONG, HOWARD. *A Profile of Mathematical Logic.* Reading, Mass.: Addison-Wesley Publishing Company, 1970. Covers the history of mathematical logic. Develops recent metalogical results and their proofs, especially as relevant to mathematics. Covers set theory and logic, philosophical implications of mathematical logic. Somewhat advanced, but a very good "profile" of the subject.

HUNTER, GEOFFREY. *Metalogic: An Introduction to the Metatheory of Standard First Order Logic.* Berkeley and Los Angeles: University of California Press, 1971. Students who have had an introductory symbolic logic course should be able to work through this book with considerable profit.

HISTORY OF LOGIC

BOCHENSKI, I. M. *A History of Formal Logic,* trans. and ed. Ivo Thomas. New York: Chelsea Publishing Company, 1970. Primarily selected historical texts. Excellent research tool.

KNEALE, WILLIAM, and MARTHA KNEALE. *The Development of Logic.* Oxford: The Clarendon Press, 1962. An impressive and somewhat unique work. Parts will be difficult for beginners. Indispensable for more advanced students.

Index